My Life...
According to the Alphabet

by

Anne Meese, MSW

Table of Contents

F

G

H

I

J

K

L

Table of Contents

S

T

U

V

W

X

Y

Z

Introduction

Like many people who are retired, I've had the gift of time to reflect and write about my life and what I've learned over my 70 years. As a result, I was able to give voice to a creative, healing process that I've expressed in my journaling for over 40 years, and that's how "My Life According to The Alphabet" came to be. By sharing my essays, poems, and stories my hope is that you'll find inspiration for continuing your own process of making peace with whatever unfinished stories you may be carrying.

Simply, the purpose of this book is the same one I had when I entered the field of mental health as a clinical social worker many years ago - to help people. My goal is to share who I am as a person in recovery - as a retired professional colleague to some, as a wife, a mother, a daughter, and a sibling.

Writing this book has meant for me:

- A reinforcement of the need for good mental health as a life long commitment. Time and time again, it opened me to the beauty of compassion I have for other people as they work to make sense of their inner lives. It also renewed in me a drive to continue practicing compassion for myself, delighting in the individual recovery work I've done.

- A sense of direction and clarity for the path I've walked in life so far. It's allowed me to get a beginning, a middle and "a preview of coming attractions" for the chapters that make up the time line of my life so far. Through my writing, I've experienced a peace regarding issues I wasn't sure I ever would, especially those around my parents. Sorting through the blocks and rabbit holes that have dogged my path for a long time has given me an affirmation and fulfillment that I'm so grateful for.

Editing 40 years of writing has been a daunting task. Hopefully, any citations I've missed will be excused. Some recovery concepts are so much a part of my thinking that after many hours of trying to decipher what is quotable and what is original to me, I can only say I've done my best with it.

I must also ask for your willingness to go with the flow of the alphabet and not a tight timeline when reading this book. I hope you can hear jazz in the individual pieces of my stories - solos, if you will - that compose a recurring melody or theme, sometimes repeating the same line. I imagine that you'll hear your own rhythm in it, at least that's my hope.

As well I hope you're inspired to use my writing as a jumping off place for your own writing. And if you're lucky like me, it might work out to be just like Wally Lamb wrote in his amazing book, I Know This Much is True*:

"The point is this: That the stream of memory may lead to the river of understanding, and understanding, in turn, may be a tributary of the river of forgiveness."

I hope that you have that kind of healing if that's what you're seeking. I hope that forgiveness works its way into your life if that's what you're working toward. I hope that you continue to be surprised and inspired by the amazing things that can happen in one day, and that when thoughts and memories circle back in your mind, you find the God of your understanding waiting there. At home. At peace.

*Lamb, Wally. <u>I Know This Much is True</u>, Harper Perennial, New York, New York 1999.

~

For my colleagues who may read this book, I hope it will be a resource to return to again and again for inspiration before you walk into a group or individual session, working to make a difference in someone's life. For the person who is new to recovery or an old timer, I wish for you the very same - inspiration and rededication to our cause, that is, to stay clean and sober one day at a time and help others to achieve recovery. And to my family and friends, I hope that reading my stories shines a light onto wherever you want to go with your own stories...and I wish you love. Lots and lots of love.

Dedication

I would like to dedicate this book in honor of two people - first, my mother, Marge, who died at age 79 in 2002, and second, my granddaughter, Margot.

She died shortly before her birth in 2012.

Mom,
I've tried to give meaning to my endeavors in life, in part, as a way of remembering you and honoring the good you carried in your heart despite hard losses, any one of which would have caused many people to give up and run away. You didn't. Instead, you stayed, keeping your family together, your main goal. Your fierce determination to make the best of what you'd been given was the best example of my life. I will be forever grateful that you were who you were and that you were my mother. My own efforts, drives, and determination come from you. To finish this book is to say thank you, Mom.

As for Margot, perhaps a poem I wrote says it best.

For Margot

So as your short life unfolded
to reveal the saddest of all endings,
we did not get to meet,
you and I,

my dear sweet girl,
my granddaughter

not in this plain
not in this time

but the good that lives and breathes over and around the
good universe
shows me who you might have been
in moments so sweet and so tender
they take my breath away
stopping time and movement
calling me to notice the scenes before me
through my longing, searching eyes

In those moments of pure grace
I imagine what might have been for you
this time around

I see you

in the faces of other children
in your father
your mother
your family.

To be honest
those connections are fleeting and few,
heart warming and heart breaking at the same time
held in a deep breath,
released in the exhale calling me back to here and now

But in some of those moments
when I get to know you from the inner world of my soul
I am changed
I am enlightened with the knowledge that
your spirit is bigger than my full heart for you
than my body
than my memory,
it's bigger than the mountains
the oceans
all the land,
it's bigger than the planets
the moon
the stars,
bigger than the Universe itself,
the Universe that holds the energy that you are, that we all
are,
using yours for the remarkable purpose
of renewing a commitment to life
for the grieving woman I am this day,
helping me tolerate a world I do not understand,
giving meaning to my years without you,
helping me find compassion for myself
and hopefully for the others I may find from the past
where miraculously I may also find the spark of you -
the spark of the divine.

My Life...

According to the Alphabet

A

Alexander and Marguerite

My parent's story is complicated. It's not an easy one to tell, especially keeping in mind that the story I tell here is only my version of events - mine as the middle of their seven children with a perspective all my own. I'm aware that not everyone in my family has the same version of events that I do.

To describe how different we are from each other, I like using the metaphor of a mobile hanging from a ceiling, with each of it's unique shapes representing a family member, open to the shifting winds that may come by, each piece being moved independently from the others. The winds that blew through my family included success, losses, calamities and traumas, comebacks and the inexplicable timing of events. These dynamics, and many more, moved each one of us in different ways, at different times, giving each one of us experiences that were uniquely ours. And so it is with this story. It is mine.

For years, the feelings I had about how things were in my house growing up were so intense that they hijacked any understanding I may have reached about my parents and the decisions they made. Any deep dive into the effects of my father's mental health issues and the reactions each one of us had to them often left me more confused than when I started. I had a lot to sort out.

However, over time, after therapy, after hours and hours in recovery groups, I was able to see my parents differently -

not as a couple, but as individuals - as people who lived through things I can only imagine. I had to admit that I don't really know what life was like for them. I have black and white photos of them from long ago and and my memories from childhood, but experience has taught me that what I've heard about memory is true - that what people believe about a given incident from the past is generally poor evidence to determine the facts of what really happened. The scenes we carry from the past are easily muddied and distorted by the passage of time, by what it was we <u>thought</u> we saw or by what it was we <u>felt</u> we'd seen. This is not to say that no one ever gets the story right, but experience has taught me that it's wise to keep the door open to interpretation when it comes to family lore.

One thing I do know for sure, though, from years of working with people who were trying to untangle their own pasts is that the decisions a person makes in life are generally influenced by many, many factors. As friends, therapists and support people, we can often only guess at what factors may be at play in any given moment for someone else. We're limited by our own perceptions, by time, by our own experiences. So, to judge my parents for the decisions they made throughout their lives that were influenced by things I'll never fully understand only sets me up as someone I don't want to be. It makes me feel righteous and arrogant when I say that they should have done this or they should have done that - like I'm better than them, and I'm not.

I'm a person who continues to seek peace with her own decisions in life, and for my parents, my wish is that they are resting in peace. I like to think that the Universe still carries their energy, and I hope that my words give them ease somehow. I will always be grateful for the lessons their lives provided me, perhaps the most impactful being that walking with someone for a while as they sift through the hard facts of their own stories, finding their own truth, can be all a person needs in that moment to find peace. Just being there for them can be enough. The answers come, the way becomes clearer - the way that once looked impossible to reason out.

For me, reasoning out my parent's story culminated in the following poem, "Because of the Nature of Things," beginning the section "Letter B."

B

Because of The Nature of Things

Because my father's family left Scotland

Because my mother's family left Ireland and France

Because they all finally settled in Cleveland, Ohio, looking for opportunity

Because they were hard workers

Because they stuck together and helped each other out

Because my grandfather, Joseph, fought and survived the horrors of WWI in 1918

Because he married an Irish girl, my grandmother, Ethel, in 1921, and they had four children

Because in 1937, Ethel died a month after her dear mother, Cora, leaving the four kids with their father, Joseph, who couldn't be counted on

Because my mother, Marge, at 15, the oldest of the four, had the courage to ask her aunt and uncle if they could live with them

Because they said yes, and brought them to their home

Because they stuck together despite the Great Depression

Because my parents met at a work party

Because my mother was an Irish beauty and a good dancer

Because my father was a handsome Scot and enjoyed dancing, too

Because WWII started in Europe in 1939

Because the US was bombed at Pearl Harbor in 1941

Because my father enlisted in the US Army in 1943

Because he had one last leave in North Carolina before he went to the fight

Because my mother met up with him there and they married

Because she waited for him to come home

Because the US won the war and he was discharged in 1946

Because everyone was told that now they could have the American dream

Because my father came back from the war a different man - angry and out of his head with drink sometimes

Because my mother had first hand knowledge from her mother about how to stay with a man like that

Because my mother had no money of her own

Because she feared for her children

Because divorce was a dirty word in the Catholic Church

Because she knew how to make the best of things

Because she would never abandon us

Because she went back to work to keep us together

Because he was getting worse

B

Because I wanted to escape

Because I needed to make a life of my own and make my own mistakes

Because my first choice of who to love was a painful one

Because I knew how to sing my pain away

Because I loved Jeff and he loved me back

Because we were given two beautiful boys by our lucky stars

Because I was theirs and they were mine

Because I knew how to stick together

Because I finished college

Because I learned about alcoholism and mental health disorders

Because I learned about my own alcoholism

Because I learned about recovery

Because I learned about the power for good in the Universe

Because things change over time

Because people change

Because of those two souls

Because love doesn't always look like love. . .

I'm here

Because of the nature of things

9

Because My Father. . .

was a puzzle to me, it took a long time to be able to see him as an individual, separate from the troubled man I knew him to be as I was growing up. When I was able to do that, I eventually found compassion for him, but not before I had to admit that I knew little of who he really was - his tastes, his talents, his goals, what he wanted out of life. There's not much information about him from family lore other than they said he was the most musically talented and the best athlete in his family of eight children. They also said he threw it away because of drinking. I knew him to be an unpredictable Dr. Jekyll and Mr. Hyde, but using the metaphor of a prism may be a better way to explain how he appears in my mind now.

The reflection of one side would show the obvious signs of alcoholism - the "ism" of it being a part of what all alcoholics and other addicted people experience to some degree. It would show mood swings, compulsive behaviors, poor decision making, defenses, fears and loneliness, physical issues, legal issues, broken relationships, broken hearts, and more.

In that reflection, there would also be the lie they tell themselves that justifies their continued use - saying that it has everything to do with other people, or work, or the government, or a war, or the weather, or a wife, a parent, a child. It's denial that makes up the lies people tell themselves so they don't have to face the ever-growing demons they are creating in their lives. The idea that alcohol and drugs could be the real source of their problems is minimized and denied over and over again. It's like being blind to what's right in front of you, never seeing all the strings that attach the drink or drug to their problems.

But turn the prism just a bit in the light, and what you'd also see is a confusing array of colors and shapes that always changed the picture of the father I thought I knew. When I was younger, this set into motion the dilemma of never knowing which steps to take around him, never sure whether he would be happy or fighting a battle in his mind. To live with that unpredictability as a child creates a mind set that, unfortunately, doesn't end with that one relation-ship, but generalizes over most relationships in the child's life to come. It becomes another facet of what's known as the family disease- a dynamic which surely existed in our home.

There would also be another facet to my father in that prism that shows a man with seven healthy kids, a wife that loved him, a home, and a good job. All the riches of a good, full life were right there in front of him. Why he didn't hold onto them is confounding, of course. I do believe he had the peculiar mental twists that are associated with symptoms of PTSD, major depression, anxiety and alcoholism, but he also may simply have wanted something other than what he already had to be happy, the grass always being greener somewhere else for someone dissatisfied with where they are. He may have just wanted out of the situation he was in.

I don't know what made up his "ism" to begin with before he started drinking - perhaps it included being blind in one eye from birth, perhaps it was the social complexities of being an immigrant to the US from Scotland. Over time, perhaps, it included what he saw in the war, or perhaps it was seeing his oldest son go to war, too, or the financial pressures of having seven kids...perhaps, perhaps, perhaps. I can only guess, knowing so little of his story. I do know about the disease of alcoholism, however, and I know it's chronic, progressive and, in his case, fatal. It kills people - whether by the direct cause of an accident, a related physical malady or by a slow day-to-day intention to kill the pain of reliving old losses and resentments, with a growing soul sickness that eventually breaks the heart - stops it cold.

I know he tried to get sober once when I was about 9 or 10 years old. I know he was helped by a group of men in recovery at the time, and by an amazing coincidence I saw one of them at a recovery conference I was attending. He remembered our family from many years before and I asked him why he thought my father struggled so with sobriety. He said, "He didn't know how to be honest." Such a simple answer for such a complicated, terrible disorder. It seemed there had to be more to it than that, but in the end, I knew the story had to start there or nothing else mattered.

The way things played out for my father will always be a sad story for me. He died a lonely death, my youngest brother being the only one in the hospital room with him to say good-bye. I hadn't seen him during the last ten years before that, never having connected with him after I left home at 19. The fear of never knowing who he'd be - Jekyll or Hyde - kept me away. That fear also kept his memory filed away in my mind for years along with anger and resentment. I was yet to learn about the many strings attaching his life to mine and yet to seek the help I needed to understand the confusing webs that had woven our family together. It was recovery that would open the door to a healing process that writing this book allows me to share with you in the pages to come.

Today I can say I'm grateful for the lessons I've learned by being his daughter, the greatest one being the ability to see the bigger picture of someone's life, from about 1,000 ft. up. Above the fray, I'm better able to take in the enormity of experiences and situations that make up the time line of someone's life and of the history of a family. Dots have to connect, and in a labor of love and the study of our family history, my oldest sister provided many of the dots I couldn't possibly have connected on my own. For her determination and heart, I'm so grateful. Thank you, sister.

Following the timeline of our family, my father's story is "to be continued," I believe. The outcomes and possibilities of how those dots might connect in the future are certainly above my pay grade. I leave that to the force of good in the Universe. When I do that, it helps me let go of what might have been. It brings me peace in the moment.

Someone once told me that God's timeline is eternity, and I like that. I like to think that for the questions I still have about my father, there might be answers in the biggest picture of all - the Universe and all that encompasses. If that's so, I hope that love is there - the love of a father for a daughter. That would be amazing.

At this age, I'm ok with what I don't know. I've spent too much of my life trying to figure out what would happen next only to learn time and again that it's a futile endeavor. Today, I know that how long anything lasts is a mystery - a life, a relationship, a lesson, a belief. It seems that the only certainty, as the Buddhists say, is that everything is changing - all the time. Understanding this has allowed me to get out of the predicting business and it keeps me curious and engaged with what's happening right now. I love that, and I'm grateful to have learned that periods of confusion and pain will eventually be followed by periods of clarity and growth - and back again as another part of the nature of things.

Being Marge...

My mother was much less a puzzle to me than my father. She was a force of nature, made of energy I've never seen in another person. She was a giver, serving her children, her grandchildren, extended family and her friends until she couldn't anymore. For a few years, like I did, she, too, participated in a mutual support group for people who've been affected by someone's alcoholism. It was the education about alcoholism and drug addiction we both received there that allowed us to share a language of hope from time to time - nothing very deep, but enough to know that she got me. She got to know what was important to me, and I got to see a deeper side to her.

From her, I was given a great lesson in the nature of how things evolve, from generation to generation, from that 1,000 ft. up. I can say it best in the following poem.

My Mom's Measuring Stick

When for years as a child I woke many school mornings from a fitful sleep
on the cusp of my parent's chaos from the night before,
the fighting words still echoing in the stairway of the bedroom I shared
with my sisters,
hoping that Mom was ok when we went downstairs...

She made us go to school,

Even though I was tongue-tied with fear for her,
scared to leave her alone,
wanting to protect her,
wanting all of us to be protected,
and wanting to tell someone that we needed help with my father,
hoping someone would save us,

We went to school

knowing that doing school work when
things were that crazy at home
was going to mean we had to follow some hard and fast rules -

1) don't talk about what was going on at home because
2) you can't trust what someone might say or do because of it, and
3) as far as feelings go, they're not important. Get over it.

It's how you look on the outside that's important.
So resigned,
I went to school.

I only saw those days of my childhood for what they were
after years of learning how to be me,
to be brave enough to feel the feelings, write the stories
and talk about them with a kind soul or two,

And I only understood my Mother's ways and
her varied solutions to the troubles we lived through together -
her strategic silences, praying the rosary,
her "business as usual" approach -
I only understood that about my Mom
when I learned about her own story
of living with a father who drank too much,
a story where she lost her mother to a weak heart,
perhaps finally broken from the fears and worries of what
would become of her four children when she finally did die,
missing the chance to raise them and keep them safe.

When I finally had a vision of my mother's face at age 15,
standing in her home with three younger siblings
watching supposed friends and family members take away
their mother's china and keepsakes after her funeral,
stealing the only parts of her they had left,

When I finally had a vision of my mother's face at 15,
struggling to keep her brothers and sister together at home,
despite being abandoned by their father,
despite him leaving them alone to fend for themselves
for days with no money,
I understood.

When one day she finally told me just a few of the stories
she carried from her childhood,
I knew what those rules were for.
I finally understood that she had a logical method
for getting past the fears and worries that come

with traumatic, life changing events.

She measured in her mind just how bad things really were.

To determine what was "bad enough" to warrant her children

staying home from school after one of their calamitous nights,

she had to measure our "present" against her "past,"

the only past she knew,

one full of such heartache and worry

that it could only paint our current events as "not that bad."

I think we all do that in our lives as we

try to decipher the truth about something or someone,

or when we try to figure out what our next move should be.

Each day we all make choices - big and small - that determine

what part we'll play in the day ahead.

For my mother,

to reason out and measure such decisions,

she followed generations of our ancestors

who made it through their own years of loss, toil and trouble.

To preserve what remained after calamity and chaos,

you followed the rules:

don't talk

don't trust

and don't feel.

Survival is what matters.

So all the while she saw things getting worse in her own
home,
and understood her powerlessness
watching her husband become sicker and sicker with drink,
caught by love and a lack of help,
she needed to know if it was time
to put on more armor
or time to laugh it off
or time to pray
or time to tend to the laundry
or time to get the kids to school
all that time
all those nights
all those days
she was measuring our troubles against the ones she had
known.

She knew about having to take a bus to get her father's
paycheck
so he wouldn't drink it away - we didn't.
She knew about having a hospital bed in their living room
for her mother who was getting sicker and sicker -
we didn't.
She knew about promising her younger siblings they'd all be
back together,
visiting them in different children's homes across town for
a year -
we never had to do that.
She knew about having to ask family members for a home -

we never knew that kind of desperation - and bravery.
She knew about loving a man who came home from war
with hidden demons and too much drink - we didn't.
She knew about putting a life aside - her's - for the love and care
and protection of her family - we didn't know about that.

She did what she always did.
She kept us together the best she could
and she knew that you have to keep moving forward,
whatever that looks like.
Even if you don't like it.
Even if it feels fake.
Even if you pray to a God you don't understand.
You make the best of whatever is in front of you to do and
you wait and see what happens.
Just keep moving forward.

She did that.
She went to school in times of chaos and confusion at home.

And in a promise to myself, as predictable as if following a script,
I tried to be different from my mom and dad, better than them -
tried to out think them, out perform them, and out run their chaos
by being the best at whatever I did.
I craved attention and to be liked by everyone,

unaware that while I was "dancing as fast as I could,"
trying to stay ahead of the storm clouds inside my home,
I was actually securing the role of black sheep in the family,
the one who didn't fit in.
And finally getting the signal that it was time to leave,
I did just that as soon as I could.

At 19, I'd left my childhood home just ahead of the years
when a new hell broke loose there,
with new threats and ramped up fighting,
and it took my brave 17 year old brother
to finally tell my beleaguered Mother how bad things really
were,
and to give my Father his cue to leave. And he did.
He died several years later, in 1982.
I never saw him after I left home in 1973.

And many years later, having learned how to stop creating
my own chaos,

I knew what to do.

I went back to school.
I got the degree
and the job,
and I created a life of my own own making
with people who loved me.

And after my parents split up and stopped making their own
brand of chaos,
it turned out that my mother

had many more remarkable chapters to live through,
some with stories of such bravery and inventiveness
they still pull me up short when retold.
I am stopped in awe at the rich, full life she made
out of what little she had,
and at the friendship she and I were able to forge between
us.
I remember her work ethic and example as a strong, single
woman,
at her ability to keep her home a welcoming place
and for the wonder that she truly was.

I know today that despite those early years of my life,
my problems as an adult have actually been of my own making
shaped by the stories I thought I needed to be safe and
smart,
shaped by my own shortcomings.

And because of that hard earned awareness,
and recovery,
and time,
and caring people who had the same story,
I taught myself to question and reflect and ask for help
when I needed to decipher the right from the wrong,
the unacceptable from the acceptable.
The real from the false.

And when I got good at that
I found a source for good in the Universe,

a source of calm and contentment,
seeing beauty in words and ideas and music,
seeing that that everything is changing and evolving,
all the time,
and that all things will eventually pass.
And once I walked around in that awareness for a while,
I saw that time has a way of evening things out,
giving meaning to the choices my mother made
and my own choices in life,
showing me the arrogance in judging any one else for theirs,
this lesson coming to me across the ages in music and stories
from a mother that was mine, a survivor, a warrior
showing me that no matter what,
I need to keep moving forward as best I can,
seeking out whatever it takes to keep at it, at life,
part of a family who did just that for generations
despite hard times
reminding me once again that I determine my next move
and how things really measure up - one day at a time.

C

The Best Thing I Ever Heard About Clinical Depression...

... was from a colleague I worked with when I was a therapist at CeDAR (The Center for Dependency, Addiction and Recovery), the treatment center in Denver affiliated with the University of Colorado Hospital. To patients that met clinical criteria for major depressive disorder who were ready to try medication, he would say that the anti-depressant he was prescribing for them was not a "fix it" or a "happy pill." He told them it wouldn't change them or their personality or the words they were going to say, but rather it might give them a chance to apply what they were learning in therapy to their daily lives. He said that by giving it a good trial run, they might find that it gave them an "ooomph" so that they could try new ways of looking at things and new ways of thinking - a powerful, hopeful message for people who had been stuck in the darkness and hopelessness of clinical depression.

Codependency

I would be leaving out a huge part of what I know about myself if I didn't write about codependency. My insights into it come from many sources - books, lectures, papers and recovery meetings. One of the most impactful sources of information for me was Dr. Tian Dayton's book, "Emotional Sobriety - From Relationship Trauma to Resilience and Balance." (Health Communications, Inc., Deerfield Beach, Florida., www.hcibooks.com).

In it, she describes the dysfunctional ways families adapt to life under the high stress of on-going emotional and physical abuse, mental illness and addiction. She explains that our brains are geared to scan for danger when we're very scared and experiencing high levels of stress. And if a person regularly experiences the feelings of overwhelm and panic that are prevalent in a chaotic home, they find they can fend off trouble by being hyper-focused on other people's emotional signals. They become very adept at reading other people's emotions, and very unfortunately, to the exclusion of knowing their own. In fact, it can become a habit for an individual to be more in touch with what other's around them are feeling than with what that individual is feeling. What was once a survival technique becomes an automatic emotional response - a habit.

Dr. Dayton explains that these habits, or patterns of behavior, are most often set in childhood and can cause complications in intimacy and parenting throughout a person's

C

life. Lacking awareness of themselves and their boundaries, the codependent person identifies how <u>they</u> feel by what they perceive <u>other</u> people are feeling. For them, sometimes it's just easier - and safer - to agree with someone else than it is to own their own thoughts and feelings.

Dr. Dayton states that <u>projection</u> is also a part of this complicated dynamic. It occurs when a person tries to change or "fix" the thoughts and feelings they perceive in someone else as being troubled when what actually<u> needs </u>to be addressed are those same troubled thoughts and feeling within themselves.

For some it's a lot like living a second-hand, giving to others for the secondary gain of being praised or rewarded for self-sacrificing behavior. It's a design for living that is dominated by feelings of deprivation and deficiency, of victimhood and the need to be rescued.

A person struggling with codependent relationships is likely to have learned at some time in their lives that if you talked about yourself, you're conceited; that giving and giving until you're depleted makes you a good person; and that to ask for anything other than what you're being given is impolite, and of course, you want to be polite - with everyone, all the time.

From this point, I could go into a cringe-worthy list of the things I did with this very mind set earlier in my life, but because I don't want to use this book for purposes of a weird confession, I can summarize the insights I've gained about those early day by using a postcard that a friend of mine brought back for me from The Louvre Museum in Paris. She said it reminded her of me. The painting is called, "St. Tresa, the Martyr." How apt... and funny, too.

C

Yes, the martyr. We were both working on our martyr tendencies at the time, and because we had a special bond
and could tease each other, I got the joke... and the lesson
in humility. A saint, I was not, and I had to take an honest
look at all the ways I was taking my identity from acts of
over-giving and over-doing. It was a hard mold to break,
and I could never have done it without my friend and others
like her in recovery.

From time to time I re-read a section or two from another
great book about codependency that I've had for over 36
years, "The Language of Letting Go," by Melodie Beattie.
This book saved me on the days I was drowning in self-
pity and the exaggerated sense I had of my impact on the
world. I thought it was my responsibility to control everything. From Melodie, I learned that by focusing on things I
couldn't control, I'd been minimizing my responsibilities for
self care. Like a passenger on a plane, I had to learn to put
the oxygen mask on myself before I attempted to help someone else - even my children. I learned that I'm truly a limited
person - like all of us. I can only help someone so much, be
there for them so much. I refer to this important book again
later under the letter V, in the essay, "Valuing The Moment."

Codependency presents a tangled web, indeed, and one I
still unravel as I continue to learn about the tendencies I
have to unwittingly use those "over" reactions to life. Still.
After all this time. Some of those messages were written
on the deepest foundational walls of who I am and I suppose they'll always creep back into my life now and then. By
being in the rooms of recovery and by reading life-changing
recovery literature, however, I've become better at addressing those old tendencies, and I've found the help I needed to

decipher what's my stuff and what isn't; what I can change and what I can't - my boundaries.

One of the best things I ever heard about keeping a healthy boundary is to look at it like a hula hoop - a safe perimeter to keep around me that holds all the good stuff I've accumulated in life - the love of my family and friends, laughter, music, funny stories, jokes, books, art, memories. It's a space that only I can devise, and I'm responsible for maintaining. And I try to remember to use it when someone in my world is being difficult and hard to get along with. I've learned that it won't cost me a thing to be kind to that person, even if for no other reason than to keep my own peace of mind. The good I keep near me in my hula hoop always outweighs the trouble at hand.

Knowing where you leave off and where someone else begins is one of the core principles of recovering from codependency, and keeping healthy boundaries is at the core of accepting the limitations you have in another person's life. Changing those old tendencies is a little like releasing your fingers from the hold you have on someone's arm, and their's on you. Finger by finger. One at a time.

Detaching yourself from the grip of someone else can be one of the smartest things you ever do in recovery. It can be the beginning of understanding who you really are, what you really want out of life, and what you believe. And when you get good at that, you'll be on new footing with yourself - now, in the present - and not with the confused reactor you once were. The wisdom you gain from knowing who you are makes the road ahead much clearer and hopefully more manageable - one change at a time.

C

The Committee

I like the use of metaphor to broaden the color and context an idea. Some good ones I've heard:

- my addiction was like a giant monster who beat me down every time I tried to get back in the ring with it.
- it felt like I had two brains - an alcoholic brain and a normal one
- it felt like everyone had the answers to the test except me.
- I was just changing seats on a sinking ship.
- I saw the writing on the wall.

I enjoy the moment when what was once confusing suddenly makes sense because I used another frame of reference to describe it. In those moments I appreciate the use of metaphor as pure art - coming right from the spirit of my creative side, providing insight into something new. It can be the spark of yet another creative endeavor - maybe a poem or a story. It's wonderful when that happens.

One metaphor that's been particularly meaningful to me over the years is the "Itty Bitty Shi@#* Committee." It's one of those ideas in recovery that gets kicked around so much that the origin of it is unknown. I only know for sure that it helped me organize the non-stop chatter and feelings of overload that hijacked my brain at times, especially early in recovery.

To make full use of it, I visualized The Committee members sitting around a table in my mind with each one named according to the emotions I was feeling at the time. The regulars - fear, anger, anxiety, worry, sadness - were there, of course, but a host of unexpected feelings like avoidance, abandonment, panic and shock could also show up. I learned to keep a seat for my inner 14 year old and a little Anne, maybe 5 years old. It could be quite a cast of characters, but they all had a chance to be heard.

From that visualization, I learned to listen to how I talk to myself - my self talk. We've all got it, this self talk. All day long we've got a dialogue going. Once I started listening to what I was saying to myself, I got much better at identifying and processing what I was actually thinking and feeling at the moment - a daunting task at times in early recovery because my mind often whirled around like a spinning hamster wheel. When I took the time - even a few minutes - to listen to what my fears were about, what I worried about or what I was sad about, etc., I found I could leave "the meeting" to face the world without high emotion and clamor in my mind. I could reason things out and move forward with clarity about what the next right thing to do might be, but it took addressing The Committee first, and that was a challenge - helpful, but a challenge nonetheless. I have to admit I was all kind of goofy to me at first, envisioning The Committee, but because it gave me a way to calm myself, I kept at it. By using the metaphor on a regular basis, I continued to learn more about thoughts and feelings in general and how to reach emotional balance in moments of overwhelm.

C

As a therapeutic practitioner of EMDR (Eye Movement Desensitization and Reprocessing), CBT (Cognitive Behavioral Therapy), ACT (Acceptance and Commitment Therapy), and Narrative Therapy with clients, I saw that understanding the various ways that self talk is connected to the past is vital to good mental health, especially if a person has high stress or past traumatic experiences that make life hard to navigate. As applied to myself, I learned that what I might be thinking and feeling about a current situation may not be accurate or related to the experience at all. It could be a replay of something that happened long ago that I just hadn't felt or reasoned all the way through*** for various reasons and was triggered once again in the present moment. Sometimes we just keep hitting replay, and sometimes it takes a good therapist to help you sort things out.

By sorting out the inner jumble and emotional disturbances of every day life, we get a chance to apply "the wisdom to know the difference" to them. That part of the Serenity Prayer is a reminder to coach myself up with what my experience shows me is true, and that worrying doesn't change a thing. I'm in charge of The Committee meeting in my head. I determine the message I'm taking from it. I'm the adult. I'm responsible for my actions and for doing my best.

Someone once handed me another great prayer in a meeting that said, "Lord, ease the pounding of my heart by the quieting of my mind" - another strong visual for the channel I try to keep open between these two most important parts of my spiritual life - my heart and mind. I hope that when your committee is holding a meeting and you're the topic (without your permission!), you can untangle the thoughts and feelings by using whatever metaphor, simile, prayer or meditation that works for you - one committee meeting at a time, one thought at a time, one feeling at a time.

God grant me

SERENITY

to accept the things I cannot change

COURAGE

to change the things I can and

WISDOM

to know the difference

D

D-I-V-O-R-C-E

Growing up in the Catholic Church I learned that divorce was a "swear word" that no one should ever say. Even Tammy Wynette wouldn't say it. She spelled it out in the title of her #1 hit song. I didn't even know what it even meant for a long time. I just knew it was bad and I should never say it. I suppose it had to do with the belief that what the priests said was true - that marriage is a sacrament given to man by God and that to break the bond of marriage is a sin, and God knows, a big one. It was that belief, I'm sure, that answered the divorce question for a lot of people. It just wasn't an option. So, being the first one in my family to get one was uncomfortable to say the least.

The simple reason it happened was because he didn't love me and instead loved someone else. When he finally got the nerve to tell me, we had been together through my senior year of high school and married 2 years - not a long time as some relationships go, but for a young person like me who was trying to get away from her family, it was a lifetime. It felt like a forever love and in a short period of time it was gone. I was devastated and humiliated, not only because there was someone else involved, but because I had to tell my mother, a devout Catholic.

With a twisted piece of logic and a good amount of pride-fulness, I had learned to protect myself from pain and dis-appointment by operating from the belief that I HAD to be better than my parents because of their marriage troubles.

I wanted to prove that I could do it the right way and have a marriage that was solid. I also wanted to prove that I could do it without help from either of them. So, when he left me and it turned out that I WASN'T any better than anyone else, all the things I thought defined me were completely gone by the time I was 23 - my home, my dog, my partner and playing music.

Little did I know I would bounce.

The couple of years following that break up turned out to be one of the most creative periods of my life. He and I had played music together as a duo and were just beginning to break into the music scene in the clubs nearby. So, I continued on that path by myself after he left, and I made my own mark on that scene. It gave me confidence and a deep understanding of what it means to put yourself out there artistically. The success I had molded the person I am today in many ways.

I found a way to get myself into college during that time. I began the journey to a degree which would take many twists and turns, but that opened the door to a world of inspiration and creativity I would never have had otherwise.

And following that break up I eventually found a new appreciation for family in the willingness of a sister to take me into her home when I'd lost mine, the willingness of a great aunt and uncle to take me into their home unannounced most evenings for the simple fun of watching "The Wheel" and "Jeopardy" and just sitting with them, and the willingness of my mother to overlook the disappointment of divorce in the family and help me as best she could.

My experience is that most committed relationships don't go bad overnight. It's true that something might happen in a 24 hour period that could be a deal breaker for sure - infidelity, relapse, physical violence, financial ruin, etc., - but mostly, the problems are there for quite a while if not from the beginning, as they surely were in my case. And whether or not the problems are clear, everyone has a different scale for what's tolerable and what's not, when it's time to say enough or time to reach out for help. Sometimes it's just too late to repair and sometimes one person just leaves.

But sometimes the love is still there after yet another "down" in the "ups and downs" of marriage. Sometimes you DO have a forever love that keeps bouncing back with a rhythm all its own, even if you've talked seriously about divorce. Sometimes the relationship can still hold and even become stronger. For me the first time around, there wasn't enough love to hold it together. There wasn't enough experience, wisdom, kindness...there wasn't much of anything but two kids trying to be adults that were better and cooler than everyone else.

It turns out that the origin of the word "divorce" is from the Old French for "divert" which means to change course. And I did and I'm grateful for it. I would never have guessed at the time that it would be the very thing I needed in order to move forward to the next part of the path I was on - a path full of adventures and being stuck, of addiction and recovery, of delights and losses. Because of this divorce, I had the chance to find out who I am, and the great good fortune to find a love that has lasted for 44 years.

"The Wedding" tells about a day in my life when I was "newly diverted."

The Wedding

Many years ago, I attended a church wedding - the whole thing, from start to finish, without anyone knowing I was there. The couple and their families were strangers to me. I never knew their names or anything about them that could possibly tie us together, yet the event is as clear in my mind today as it was that day.

Back then I was the singer in a band that used the church sound studio for rehearsals, and one Saturday afternoon I was early for our scheduled time.

I was climbing the stairs to the second floor when I heard Sting's "Fields of Gold" being played on a piano from the church below, so I inched my way into the nearby balcony and perched myself on a bench, hidden, with a bird's eye view of the whole church and the beginning moments of the ceremony.

Right away, I questioned my new found voyeurism, wondering if I should leave, but after a few minutes I couldn't pull myself away, feeling that I somehow needed to be there. So, I settled in to my dark corner, determined not to be found out and took in the whole beautiful scene.

First, the groom made his appearance from the right side of the altar followed by his groomsmen, forming a distinguished line of tuxedoes. The bridesmaids came down the aisle soon afterward in a slow parade of shimmering blue and silver, forming their line on the left.

D

Then, as the crowd of about 100 stood and turned toward the center aisle, the elegant "Pachelbel's Canon in D" filled the church, and there she was, the bride, simply beautiful - even from behind, on the arm of a stately someone, likely her father, the two of them making their way slowly to the front, the future waiting for her there.

The memory of that experience is triggered for me every once in while, by what, I can't predict. But each time it is, I wonder about that bride and how things turned out for her. I wonder if she lost herself like I had to the husband who had only recently left me, so close to the time she was joining her's.

Hopefully, she knew who she was and didn't lose herself in the process of becoming a couple. Maybe she held onto her dreams. Maybe she didn't hold herself back and wait for her turn. Maybe she just knew to step up and take it when the timing was right.

My own wedding day, just about two years before, was nothing like this couple's. I was a young girl, really - desperate for love above all else, and by then very used to the painful twisting and turning that my husband-to-be and I did to each other well before we even got to our civil ceremony in the local mayor's office.

One thing I do remember from that day, sadly, was that I was floating on air, ecstatic under the delusion that everything would change if we got married. Whatever it was that initially held us together easily came apart in the end, as delusions often do - with tears and fears about the future and beginning an entirely new life at age 23.

To close this couple's ceremony, the pianist filled the church with "Jesu, Joy of Man's Desiring," and I watched as the happy couple walked down the aisle and out of the church, their guests applauding and following them to the party waiting for them, no doubt.

It was a joyous event, my joy for them a secret, of course. I was a spy, after all, holding a grateful silence to have been there, solitary in my awe and confounded at how adventures like their's truly begin, hoping one might be ahead for me, never guessing that I was to have another wedding day of my own in a few years, with genuine love and a long term marriage, with many chapters to live and stories to tell, and one about a Saturday afternoon I was held fast to some secret moments by the feeling of hope and love on the way, and the possibility of happiness once again, grateful to see it in such a grand display that day, and in my mind's eye, even now.

E

Ego

I have a friend in recovery who talks a lot about the ego and addiction. She says that if the time comes that you're being easily offended by people, your ego is usually too big. I like that.

It speaks to the idea of the "double life" that the alcoholics and addicts I've met over the years so often identify with. The person's ego gets over-sized as they continue their attempts to show the outside world how great they're doing when in actuality that facade doesn't match the emotional pain they're feeling on the inside. They have a desperate need to hide their insecurities and sensitivity by acting like, "I don't care what you say about me," when they actually do care - a lot. Trying to control hurt feelings by hiding them behind the bravado of the ego is not the solution. In the end, they're only fooling themselves.

What's the antidote when you're feeling super sensitive and you realize that your ego is in control? Following are some acronyms I've heard in recovery groups that might help:

EGO -

Edging
God
Out

In other words, you might be feeling overly sensitive and reactive because you're being shown something you don't want to see, so you do what you can to ignore or avoid the truth about it.

FAITH -

Finding
Answers
In
The
Heart

By listening to your self-talk, you may be able to get to past the intense feelings of the moment and tune into what's going on in your heart, your gut and intuitive thoughts and feelings. Giving a listen to the great Stevie Wonder song, "Have a Talk With God," (from the album, "Songs in The Key of Life") might be an inspiration, too.

Take HOPE -

Hearing
Other
People's
Experiences

The ego wants to say you're right and the real problem is how other's are treating you, but finding the courage to get feedback from someone else about the situation can be a great help - even when it's something you don't want to hear.

Realizing that you've actually been in control of very little - especially other people - can be humiliating, but you need not stay there - in humiliation. It can also be humbling in that human, freeing way that says everyone else is limited, too, and you're not alone - even in the mistakes you make. It's a truth that's not always easy to accept, but one that can shine a light on how much time we waste on hiding behind ego.

Once the ego is "right-sized," I believe I have a chance at true humility and acceptance of the fact that I don't need the smoke and mirrors of a double life. Being human and in sync with myself is the easier, softer way and I choose that today.

Expectations

"I don't think anyone would be interested in reading about my family,"

said the seasoned poet in an interview I read.

"Well," I thought to myself, "I'm screwed because that's all I write about."

But wanting to be like him, I began writing about "topics" and "subjects,"

only to get lost in the weeds with my well-worn opinions and ideas.

Then I read a memoir by a successful writer I admire in which

she basically told my whole story.

Down to the alcoholic father. I couldn't tell it any better than that.

"What a story!" I said. "Drat!!"

I was stuck.

Then one day I heard a famous author give a talk about creativity, and she said, in effect,

Screw all that chatter in your head. Write because you enjoy writing.

E

Just start, and what you'll end up doing with it will come in time. Just start and don't stop. Then she said,

Just create art for the sake of art, for the enjoyment of it, and the new vision of the world it affords you.

And that changed everything.

I got out of my own way and put pen to paper again,

and I kept writing until I was done that day.

Then I did it the next day, and the next, and the next...

I stopped expecting what would happen

if I really started living the life I wanted - as an artist, a writer, a musician.

If I was scared or blocked or confused

I did it anyway

no matter what I felt like creating that day

and I waited to see what happened

and I learned that was enough to call it a good day

and to call myself an artist.

I found my voice

past the doubt,

past my perceived expectations of others,

past the worry of not being accepted,

past the fear of sharing myself.

And in meditation

I thanked the seasoned poet, the memoirist and the successful author

for the challenge they posed to me,

and then I kindly showed them the door,

and returned to myself

to my writing

but first, to sing a song or two

Expectations

an essay

Many years ago, my dear friend, Pat, taught me a great lesson about expectations and how mine needed adjusting. I've shared one of her stories many times over the years and want to share it here as well.

She said that one night she was talking to a good friend about coming home from work every night and having the same fight with her kids because they didn't start the chores. She'd walk in the door to find once again that no one had started dinner, the house was a mess, no one was doing homework, the TV was on, etc. The repeating scenario was that she'd usually loose her temper, everyone would scatter and then she'd end up stomping around in anger and frustration, doing the chores she had wanted them to do.

She said that her friend then asked her what it was that she really wanted to do after work, and she told her she'd love to just lay down for 15 minutes to relax before her evening started. Her friend said that nothing was going to change if she kept doing the same thing over and over again, and she suggested that Pat take time for that 15 minutes after work the next day.

So, she said, the next day, she came home from work to find it in the usual disarray it always was when she got home from work, but this time she just said a quick "hi" and walked upstairs to lay down. By the time she took off her shoes and laid down on the bed, the uproar downstairs started. One was yelling at the other to start dinner, another one was yelling about putting things away, and someone turned off the TV and started yelling about doing homework.

She called her friend, holding out the phone and said, "Listen to the yelling!" and her friend said, "Good - that's what change sounds like." She said her friend challenged her to finish her 15 minute break and then calmly go downstairs - regardless of what she saw that the kids did or didn't do. She said if you can do that, change will happen - you just don't know <u>how</u> it will happen.

Pat said she didn't know if the kids thought they'd pushed her over the edge or what, but whatever the reason was, the chores were eventually done - not necessarily as <u>she</u> would have done them, but rather as <u>they</u> would. And she kept at this new practice with incrementally better results, making progress without perfection. The kids got the message on their own most of the time and she was calmer and more relaxed after a hard day at work.

The lesson I took away from Pat is that changing priorities and expectations can be loud, messy and generally make a lot of noise - even if it's only in my head. It can be crazy-making, but if I've made a good plan, if it feels right for the moment AND I stick to it, the outcome can be for the better. Mostly, I just need to try. If I don't try, things will never change.

Her story was about being able to react in new ways. What a great "real time" lesson for those kids, too, to see the example of a person who can change. Pat was a smart person and a terrific mom. I had the chance to meet a few of her kids once. They were helping out at a Christmas party she was having - the pay off of good parenting and being open to change. Thanks, Pat.

F

Filters

I went to Cleveland State University in Cleveland, OH, for my undergrad and graduate degrees in social work as a non-traditional student - a nice way of saying I was older (I got my masters degree at 50). I was definitely in the minority - both as an older student, but also a white student.

I never really fit into the mostly black campus community there, but I wasn't really there for a college experience, per se. By then I had a busy life in recovery, two teenagers and a husband at home, and I lived across town. I dug into my studies, did research, wrote papers, completed two internships, and a graduate assistant position in my senior year. They asked me back to teach a semester in the masters class. I received a good education there because I put a lot into it. I learned how to think like a social worker, and I believe my experiences there made me a better person. One lesson I came away with from a fellow student who was black is something I keep with me still.

She was in the same group of students I was in that shared with each other how our internships were going. One day she told us that when she was at her's in a nearby hospital, she had to use what she called "filters," and she explained what they were. She said that she'd been taught in her family from an early age to hate white people - her words. She was told to never talk to them if she could help it and never to trust them - that they were only out to hurt her - and this was repeated to her over and over again as she grew up.

Then she saw that things didn't really measure up that way when she was out in the world away from her family. She said that when she started going to school and working around white people that message in her head was confusing and simply untrue. She found that race had nothing to do with who was going to be nice or mean to her, who was helpful or not. So, she said, she started to use what she called a filter in her mind to remind her that all white people were not out to get her. She said that filtering for her was a process of removing those unwanted statements from her mind so she could assess the situation objectively and get to know people before making judgements about them. She wasn't complaining about it and instead said that using a filter was just a fact of life for her.

At first, I thought how sad it was that her parents were coming from a place of such fear that they felt they needed to keep her safe in that way with those messages. Then I thought I'd probably have done the same thing, knowing myself how unsafe the world can be. I can only guess how I would have raised my children in that situation.

The lesson I took away from my colleague was how important it is to set aside any preconceived judgments I may have about someone when I first meet them. I need to filter them out, just like she did. I don't want to be ruled by fear, and starting out my interactions with others in a spirit of curiosity and kindness is how I want to be. It doesn't make me a saint. It's just the easier, softer way to live.

If I'm honest with myself, I know I have prejudices - I was raised with them and they're written on the walls of my mind. It's my responsibility to be aware of them, however,

F

and filter them out as I get to know someone as an individual instead of walking on eggshells around them, wondering if my preconceptions about them could be true.

Using my own filter has worked for me many times and I'll always be grateful that she shared her hard-earned lesson and practice. I hope she is doing well and continues to help others filter out the unnecessary limits we put on ourselves and others.

Forgiveness

I read an article years ago about a priest from South Africa who told a story about forgiveness that helped me understand it as I never had before. He said that one day during the time of apartheid in his country, he received a letter bomb in the mail that blew his hands off when he opened it. When asked by the journalist if he thought he would ever accept an apology from the person who did this to him if it ever came about, he answered yes, he would, but added that he'd ask the person for something in return after accepting it.

He said that what would mean more to him than an apology, was this person's willingness to help him with the tasks of daily living since everything was so hard without the use of hands, like dressing, tying his shoes, bathing, cooking, etc. He explained that because his main goal since the explosion was to live without the bitterness and hatred that could consume him if he let it, he had already forgiven the perpetrator as a purposeful act of grace. He said that he knew if he truly wanted to live his best life, he didn't have a choice but to forgive them. He said he's already made peace with himself about not needing an apology in order to move forward with his life, so that if one happened to come along, the words would be secondary in importance to receiving the help he very much needed.

I love the practicality of his answer and the idea that what is just as meaningful as the words we say to each other, maybe even more so when making amends, are the actions we take to improve the conditions between us. I've heard that making an amends is not complete unless you ask the person to whom you're apologizing if you've missed anything that needs mending and if there's anything you could do to mend the break that occurred. I like the complete circle of that.

In making amends that I've owed to other people during my life, I've found that people mostly want their hurt feelings acknowledged. They want to know that I realized I hurt them. Having been the recipient of amends during my life, I know how healing that can be in and of itself. But if you're lucky enough to be given the chance as I have to "live" the amends, in small ways every day through changed behaviors and a kindness done quietly without the need for thanks, you may also know forgiveness as I have. Rather than a moment of cleansing, I found it to be this slow and steady stream, imperceptible until a moment comes along when you know you've been changed for the better - for others and for yourself. You been softened.

May you find that river of forgiveness as you continue to live imperfectly - just like me.

What Forgiveness Sounds Like

What asking for forgiveness can sound like:

- I'm honestly sorry for...(with no excuses or explanation why - no "but I...")
- Please accept my apology.
- I'm making changes so I don't do the same thing again.
- Is there any way I hurt you that I've missed?
- Is there anything I can do to make this right?
- Is it ok if I sit here with you for a while?
- I'll go now.

What forgiving someone else can sound like:

- Thank you.
- I accept your apology.
- I understand.
- I know you tried.
- I see that you've changed that.
- Let's begin again.
- May you find peace.
- Let's move on.

F

What forgiving myself can sound like:

- I'm worthy of forgiveness.
- I didn't know how to save myself back then and I'm sorry for that.
- I didn't know how to help myself. I know now.
- I wasn't strong enough to change back then. I am now.
- I'm sorry I said I hated myself. I don't.
- Breathe in forgiveness. Breathe out shame.
- I'm so glad to be back here.

G

The Gift of Choice

The metaphor I like to use to describe my alcoholism is a can of Campbell Soup. I already had the "ism" in the can before I took a drink. I just needed to add the liquid, alcohol, to make it "soup," so to say.

A big part of my "ism"_includes how I was raised and what my home was like growing up. As I've shared earlier in this book, my father was an active alcoholic who needed help and my mom was a little Irish gal who had no where else to go with 7 kids. They had each lived through horribly traumatizing experiences during their lives that no doubt made up at least part of the framework that contributed to their troubles with each other and that spilled over onto their children in various ways. To be raised in a home like that, that revolves around addiction and trauma, is a prescription for adjustment and attachment issues for the kids. No one gets out of those family systems without some degree of trauma themselves. The webs those dynamics weaved are all a part of my "ism."

Besides where and how I was raised, however, is another part of my "ism" which includes the characteristics that most people in recovery are familiar with from literature and meetings. How they played out in me included:

Resentments: I thought that staying mad at someone - resenting them and what they did - was a smart thing to do as a defense against being hurt again.

<u>Low self-esteem/huge ego</u>: I had a civil war going inside myself between two beliefs. On one hand I thought that if you really knew me you wouldn't like me VS. the opposing thought that I was desperate for you to know me and like me.

<u>People Pleasing:</u> I thought that if you liked me, then I liked me, so it was imperative that I kept you happy.

<u>Higher Power</u>: I had a Santa Claus relationship with God, begging for what I wanted, but never knowing how to please God enough to get it.

I had all of that going on before I had my first drink at 15 years old.

To describe the progression of my alcoholism, I like using the visual of a series of plateaus, each one descending lower and lower, more dangerous and different from the previous one. Regardless of the circumstances, the people, places or things in each one, I was headed in one direction - down - when I was drinking.

My first drinking plateau was mostly uneventful. It included that first drink at age 15 with friends one night. I loved it. It was the first time I felt relaxed and I knew right away why it was that people drank - for that calming effect and the feeling that everything was all right. Fortunately for me, I was also scared by it because of what alcohol was doing to my family, so I only drank a few times in high school and it wasn't a big part of my world for a few years after that.

I was cautious around alcohol on that plateau because I was determined to never be like the alcoholics I knew. I was

G

going to drink, I knew, but I was going to do it differently - not like them. I was never going to need it like they did. Besides, I had another obsession and compulsion - my high school boy friend. I thought that he was all I needed and that he and I would show everyone else how a relationship should work AND be cool doing it. A chance I had to attend college fell through, so a future with him became the plan and we decided to marry.

My drinking still stayed in that occasional range until the time he decided there were greener pastures for him without me and we divorced. I found that the plateau I had been on up to that point was no longer going to work for me. I lost a lot in that break up and was devastated. I had burned a lot of bridges to be with him and found myself at age 23 alone and firmly into my role as black sheep of the family. I was on my own, starting a new chapter - and I descended to a lower plateau.

Remarkably at first on this new setting, many good things happened for me. I was able to make a busy, full life of playing music, working and going to college. It was a new and creative environment and I was thriving in many ways. And while I was still mindful of what alcohol could do to a person, I told myself that drinking would be different for me, that I was smart enough to keep out of trouble with it. I never had hangovers if I did drink a lot on occasion and It didn't really affect my daily life.

What I did not foresee, however, was how it was becoming a part of my life. I loved drinking at night alone in my apartment and looked forward to it during the day, like you might look forward to seeing a good friend. I came to count on how it made me feel. I told myself it was a reward for all I was doing during the day. I told myself it relaxed me. I told myself it helped me think more clearly. I told myself it made my music sound better. I told myself it helped me fall asleep, but the truth was that it helped me pass out every night.

I didn't notice that it was more than just the way I ended my busy day. I didn't see how I had come to depend on those nightly drinks to handle the eventual painful reminders of what I had lost. I tried to forget the sadness and stress in my life by escaping into a drink. I hid most of my grief during the day with busyness, with lots of people, in different places, doing new things. Because I was young and eager, I showed people during the day that everything in my life was great and that I was doing great. Just great.

I understand that the reason most people drink is for entertainment, for fun, sociability and a good time, and I certainly had a good measure of that during those years, but I also had no discernible consequences for the drinking I was doing alone. It only lead me to drink more - and need more to feel like I wanted to feel. I was convinced it was helping me, and I justified it by measuring my drinking against the drinking of people I thought were obviously alcoholics. It never crossed my mind that I could be like them, even though my drinking was increasing. On this plateau, it still wasn't interfering in my daily life or my goals for the future. I didn't get any DUIs, I was supporting myself doing what I loved and I had a lot of friends. However, even though I wasn't aware of it, I was inching downward onto another plateau.

G

I finally dropped to that next plateau when I got into a faster lane of life with a drinking partner, this cute guy I met in a club one night, my husband today. From the get go, it was clear that we both wanted more out of life, and clear as well was that the setting for it was going to include more drinking. No longer drinking alone at night, the point of working, going out, having friends, etc., changed from the reward I was giving myself at the end of the day to drinking every day because that's how you squeezed more out of it.

The disease of alcoholism for us just looked different from any other example I'd seen before. We married after 10 months and I thought the life I had pursued on my own could be duplicated wherever it was we were going. The pursuit of more and increased drinking, however, lead us into an awful dynamic that is defined very well in the recovery pamphlet, "The Dilemma of the Alcoholic Marriage." It describes the merry-go-round of drinking and denial. There's a cycle we were caught in that went like this: drinking = trouble = denial = adapting to it by changing yourself, avoiding conflict, minimizing...then it continues - drink = trouble = denial = adapting and so on. In the morning, I'd wake and worry that we needed to do more than drink and work, and I'd tell myself that we were going to talk about things that tonight...except our talking about things that mattered would start with drinks and we'd be bickering and fighting by the end of the night.

And we did that for years.

There wasn't much I did without a drink somewhere in the picture on that plateau, and I stayed there for years, moving farther and farther away from the goals I had for myself, making important life decisions - like dropping out of school, marrying and having children, moving - in pursuit of more as I slowly but surely moved down to the next plateau.

The next one was the most difficult and last one I would experience. It was in our home with our children and dogs and neighbors and schools and parties - a full life on the outside, but still masking the depression and anxiety I had about the home we were making behind the scenes. I no longer thought of having a drink as a choice - it was just part of what I did. The mental obsession to drink had turned into full blown preoccupation and the physical cravings were always just under the surface making sure a drink was going to happen.

We had made a big life for ourselves at that time. It included starting businesses, financial success, buying and selling several houses, big parties and drinking friends. We looked great, too. We had the house, the cars, the vacations, the lifestyle. We had the more we had been pursuing.

This stage held the fondest memories of my life, raising our boys, but it also had the darkness of daily drinking and denial about the way I parented and the way I partnered with my husband. Thankfully, we had no blow out fights and no DUIs between us, but all anyone needed to do was scratch the surface of that picture I'd been trying to fit everything into, and beneath it was something quite different.

We were in the same cycle we'd always been, only now it was going faster and faster. I was an emotional wreck and needed alcohol by then. I was anxious all the time about what was happening with my drinking because of what I'd

G

seen my parents go through. I knew it was getting worse. I tried to control it at times limiting how much I drank, but to no avail. I was constantly worried about the kids being around our bickering and fighting and tension all the time. My parenting style consisted of being strict and thinking things had to be perfect followed by guilt and over-giving to them. The daily drinking that started around supper time started earlier on the weekends. I had alcohol on my breath every time I kissed the kids good night. I had to try not to slur my words. I had terrible hangovers and I had terrible boundaries with other people. I had overwhelming fears of becoming "that mom" in the neighborhood which only increased my desire for perfection. And I was terribly depressed, angry and anxious - sometimes all at once.

So what happened was...

I saw a cousin of mine at a family party who told me about some recovery meetings she was attending and how she thought they might help me after I had told her my tale of woe about how other people were drinking - not me. Because of the seed planted by my cousin, after a few weeks I attended a recovery group for family and friends of alcoholics and as the Universe would have it, a woman alcoholic in recovery was the speaker that night. She basically told my story - not exactly the same; we had different life experiences, but she said enough for me to know I needed to look at my own drinking. I knew right then and there I was going to have to stop, but the prospect of what would have to change froze me in my tracks. I didn't see how I could pull it off. My introduction to recovery that night only served to change my usual drinking into "guilt drinking" - the worst way to do it. It's when the relief is no longer there and every drink just makes you feel worse. I was in a miserable, frightening place.

My fears and the vision of where I was headed eventually lead me back to that meeting and more meetings. I would go late and leave early, thinking that if I just found out how those people managed not to drink, I could do it, too. I took notes during the meeting because I thought I'd figure out how to do it on my own. Then I finally got scared enough and, as a good friend of mine says, I was sick and tired of being sick and tired. It was as if I had been descending the side of a mountain for a long time, and by starting a program of recovery I was being offered a second chance - one where I could turn and step off that last plateau.

The day I finally surrendered and admitted to someone else that I needed help with my drinking, I started down a different path. By then, thankfully, the landscape was not entirely unfamiliar to me. That "closet recovery" I was doing alone for three years following my initial meeting — by reading recovery literature and books, taking notes, going to meetings, thinking I could control it - helped me understand "recovery speak" a bit better so that I didn't feel so lost in the woods with all of it. I'll never know why I finally listened to the message I heard in my head that day in Bethany Beach at the end of a hectic, stressful vacation, but I did. The message was that how I was living was insane and that I needed to go back to the women I'd met in recovery meetings. After being honest about my drinking with one of them, I felt I was finally in recovery for real, and that made all the difference.

I had enough willingness to let in the truth and enough openness to be teachable. By then, I was ready for a new way of life - the spiritual way of life described by people in recovery who had gone before me. I saw in their eyes that they had made peace with their pasts and were fully alive in the present. They knew the way to serenity - something I had never experienced before - and it kept me coming back to meetings.

I followed a daily routine that started with choosing not to drink for one hour at a time, one day at a time and not picking up that first drink, no matter what. I followed the simple suggestions I heard at meetings about how to stay sober - suggestions that were equivalent to putting on my own oxygen mask before anyone else's. I didn't have to believe in anything religious either. People told me to believe in my own concept of the Higher Power that would help me stay sober. They also didn't want to hear about my politics. Mostly, the people I was meeting were kind and friendly. That's what kept me wanting to come back to the next meeting and be a part of the group.

I was lucky enough to be the youngest in a group of mature, achieving sober women that I wanted to be like. Because I've always been a good copier, I learned to "act as if," or basically, to copy them and act like I thought they would. I had some growing up to do and they were my teachers.

During the day, I'd wonder how they would act in a given situation, and I'd try it out. I had many great examples from them. One thread that ran through all of their stories, however, was that no matter what happened they weren't going to drink that day. So, I said the same thing, and eventually it got easier and easier not to think about the first drink until I could go for longer and longer periods without thinking about it at all. I told myself it wasn't an option any more because to me it wasn't.

If it happened that I couldn't go to a meeting or meet someone for coffee on a give day, I learned how to coach myself up with a slogan, to say a prayer, or journal. I learned how to do a simple check in with another sober woman on the phone. And once I got better at using these tools of the program, I truly learned about the gift of choice. Having gotten past the cravings and mental obsessions that had once ruled my day, I could choose to stay away from the first drink until I didn't drink because I didn't want to drink.

By continuing to do the next right thing, the next kind thing in front of me to be done - and some days just not making things worse - I started to see the many choices I had in front of me to build a fulfilling life. And because I chose to evolve and grow along those same lines, I also chose to finish college and get a masters degree, and I chose the career I wanted, and I chose friends that were good for me, and I chose to believe there is a Higher Power that works for good - all of these and more made up the second chance I'm given every day in recovery. The better choices I started making for my life at age 38 continued to turn my sobriety into the new landscape I still walk today. No longer limited to a small plateau, I walk the path of recovery today with my husband who, amazingly, got sober, too.

We had to learn how to do things differently in recovery. We had to learn how to live as sober individuals, as a sober couple and as sober parents. And we had a lot of help.

We went to therapy, we went to meetings, we made new friends - mutual friends and friends of our own. We had sober parties. And most importantly, we learned how to handle life on life's terms. We were able to be there for our kids through crisis when they needed us. We've been there for friends and family as well.

Because I practice my own separate program from my husband, I learned how to be independent within my marriage to him. I'm my own person and I know myself today. We're both happily retired now and still work from the premise that I have a side of the street that is all mine and he has one that belongs to him. I'm responsible for my side - my life, my interests, the things I like to do - and he is responsible for his. That makes coming together a sweet thing. We share what's happening on our individual sides when we want to. Sometimes during the day I'll invite him onto my side and ask him to listen to me read something I've written. Sometimes he'll invite me into a project he's working on. This process works well for us.

I go to more recovery meetings than I ever did. I go because I never want to drink again and I need the "insurance" they give me so I won't. I go because that's where my friends are, and I go because I still have flaws and character defects that can block my way forward. I think I'll always need help with that, cutting back the vine, as I've heard it said.

As far as my spiritual life goes, I like to say I have a deep and abiding faith...that comes and goes. And over time I've learned that's how it's going to be for me. It's a bit like having a Higher Power that's a grandmother who sends me off into the world to live my life and eventually return to her with my tales, finding her excited to see me, dedicated to supporting me. There's no guilt in that relationship. If I ever become aware that I'm in an emotional twist, trying once again to do life alone, all I have to do is return to what I know - with no shame - to my intuition, my inner calm, the center of who I am and the connection I have to something that's greater than me in the Universe - the Higher Power.

Early sobriety may not feel like a choice when your body, mind and spirit have been off balance for so long. The restlessness and irritability of one day can feel endless. I remember wanting to jump out of my skin many times. To learn how to calm myself was a huge accomplishment and I did it by going to meetings and practicing what I've shared here. I had to learn how to stop the hamster wheel in my head and calm myself down before I could dig into the real work of self-reflection and self-discovery that a life in recovery asks for. I keep at it because of the many gifts I receive as a result of continuing to choose not to drink today. And why would I? I don't want to miss a thing.

About Grief

In moments of reflection when I can reach beneath the surface of the angst or irritation I might be feeling, I find it's often the small, hard stone of grief locked in my chest. Once acknowledged, I find the words of loss there, waiting to be written or spoken, the tears waiting to be cried. It's surprising to me how often it's grief that's there - that deep, hidden sorrow - at the core. It could be about a recent loss or one I experienced years ago. It could be about something big or something small. I've heard a lot of people say that these feelings of grief occur more often as you age. I'm not sure about that, but understanding my own grief has lead me to some guideposts I try to remind myself of when it comes around again:

Don't romanticize the painful thoughts by replaying the tape in your mind of how you wish things could have been. Eventually, it only brings more pain and it changes nothing.

Everyone handles pain differently, so don't compare your grief to someone else's. You can only imagine what someone else might be going through in a given moment. You'll never know exactly. There's just too much data in that file.

Remember that there have been times when your heart was breaking, but you still went to the party or the meeting or the grocery store, etc. You can still function and be hurting. You're strong enough to do that.

Remember that the pain will pass - your mind and body just can't sustain it that long. You will smile again, and...

If you linger too long in the pain, self-pity could be close by, and for people in recovery that's an awful place to be. Recognize it for what it is, coach yourself up with self-love and share it with someone else if you can't get past it. Then hand it off to the Universe. Let it go and see what happens.

It may still hurt after you let it go. Losing someone or something you really wanted is about the hardest thing to get past in life, but take hope. The Universe has a way of evening things out and reminding us that grief is normal. It's normal human stuff that everyone experiences. It says you're alive.

Gut

I've always been in awe of people who seem to know how to do and say the right thing as I'm stumbling over my words or misreading the situation. My good friend, Mary, was a lot like that. She was dignified and gracious and had what seemed to be an intuitive sense of how to be herself with other people.

That intuitive sense - or intuition - has always been an interesting topic to me and I've come to some conclusions about it. I've found that my intuition doesn't speak to me in words or phrases. It speaks to me through my gut and how it feels when I'm thinking about doing something. It gives me direction and a sense of:

what I have to accept
what I can change
when it's time to go
when it's time to lean in
who is genuine
who is not
where it's safe to be
where it's not...

I think those answers sit right there - in the deepest part of me - my core. And the more I listen, pray and meditate from that center space within me, the more I know myself - whether in calm or tension, serenity or concern.

I think it's cool that the word for God in German is "Gott," pronounced "gut." Learning this gave me a deeper connection to my spiritual life. It's a strong sense of knowing that I'm connected to the wisdom of experience - mine and others. The next right thing, and next kind thing to do is there, too. It's all right there. My gut tells me so.

H

Healing

You can grieve and still be ok. You can feel the anger and guilt that goes with it and it won't kill you. You can breathe through it. It is endurable. The following dialogue from the movie, "Wind River," expresses that so well. The character played by Jeremy Renner said to his friend played by Gil Birmingham whose daughter was murdered:

"A counselor came up to me and sat down next to me. He said something that stuck with me -

He said, "I got some good news and some bad news.

The bad news is that you'll never be the same.

You'll never be whole. Not ever again.
You lost your daughter and nothing is ever going to replace that.

The good news is that as soon as you accept that
and let yourself suffer,
you'll allow yourself to visit her in your mind
and you'll remember all the love she gave,
all the joy she knew.

You can't steer from the pain.
If you do you'll rob yourself of every memory of her.
Every last one.
From her first step to her last smile.

You'll kill 'em all.
So take the pain.
That's the only way you'll keep her with you."

Written and directed by Taylor Sheridan
"Wind River," distributed by Lionsgate, 2017

What I take away from such wise, beautiful words is that there isn't a group or person or idea - nothing - that will ever make up for or take away the pain of losing a family member or friend. If you try to ignore it or out run it, it comes out in weird ways, in weird, disjointed conversations, in weird comments, and in weird feelings that don't seem connected to anything relevant in the moment. It can make you a little crazy from all the twisting and turning you have to do to deny it.

But if you can fully acknowledge and feel it all the way through, in that moment you are honoring it, her, him, them...and it can be transformative. You can be healed in the ways all people are - inexplicably from within, by the power for good in the Universe, given to us as part of our humanity and what connects us to each other. You can find again that which was once lost. It will be in a memory, in a picture, in a song...in a new day.

Hero

The boy on the TV news was all smiles, beaming with pride, recognized as a hero at age 10 by the local Fire Marshall for having saved his family from a house fire that happened in the middle of the night. I was all smiles for the little guy, too, being a young mother at the time and imagining what a gift he was to his family.

Then it hit me like a flash. I had done the same thing, at just about his age, and after a bit of reflection the story came back to me.

I remembered that my father fell asleep in the living room chair with a lit cigarette and it caught on fire. I woke up to the smell of smoke in the upstairs bedroom I shared with my 4 sisters.

I ran downstairs and found my father throwing a pan of water on the burning chair. He yelled to me to get my mother. I woke her, and she ran out of the bedroom, joining my father in the frantic actions of trying to put out the fire.

I ran back upstairs and woke my sisters. Then I ran downstairs to the basement and woke my two brothers. We all got out safely and went to the back yard, unable to see what our parents were doing to put out the fire at the front of the house.

Triggered by news of this young boy's experience, I also remembered something else from that night.

I remembered that when all seven of us were huddled together in the dark of the backyard, sitting around the picnic table, strangely, I couldn't have been happier and I didn't want it to end. I felt safe there, sitting together, with my older brother making jokes and telling stories. We were laughing and goofing around the way that only siblings can, distracted from the frightening unknown that was just around the corner.

I don't remember how long we stayed there, but I do remember my mother calling us in, saying something like, "It's all over now. Go back to bed." I remembered filing back in the house smelling of smoke and getting a glimpse out the front door to see the smoldering, black chair with the garden hose on the ground nearby. I also remembered that the chair was gone by the time we went to school in the morning, and the only sign that anything had happened the night before was a small burnt spot on the lawn,

and...

I can't recall one time that we ever spoke about that night in my family. Not even the next day. I hadn't even thought of it until I saw the story on the news that day.

That's what happens when one of the rules in your family is that you don't talk about what's going on in your house to anyone, because, the warning goes, you can't trust anyone, but more importantly, YOU will bring shame on the family if you do. Not the person who caused the problem. YOU will. You're supposed to keep it to yourself and forget about it.

So I did.

And life went on after that night and many more like it, as it does in families with unaddressed, volatile issues - with one unpredictable incident after another and the reminder to keep it to yourself. What can happen with openness and willingness in recovery, however, is that a person begins to realize there are mental strings that attach those early experiences to present day experiences. Sometimes they affect us in small ways - from person to person in how we speak to each or what we share - or they can affect us in powerful ways such as in my childhood memory of the fire that night.

Through the healing processes of recovery that I share in this book, my brain was changed with new connections from the past to the present, and it became fertile for the awakenings that can happen by just being aware of life around me, fertile for moments like I experienced hearing that boy's story. And by learning more about the past, I found the thread of my own voice. And with it, I learned to sooth myself and settle the questions and conflicts I had carried for so long.

I learned to talk to that little 10 year old girl that I was. I told her I thought she was brave and that she was a good daughter, and that I know she always tried her best. I told her what a remarkable gift she was to her family that night for saving them, and that I would never forget what she did. I thanked her for saving us, and I told her I was glad that we were together today. I have said those words, in different forms, many times to coach myself up in my life, and I committed to saying them to that scared child I was if she ever appears in my fears again.

And as life went on and the fates would have it, I worked in the mental health field for 20 years, helping others find their voices to take the steam out of their stories and make peace with the past. Doing that work, I found that even though the faces and places may be different, the stories we all carry are very similar, and I was lucky enough to see the value in my own stories and how to use them to help someone else.

And then it happened that one day early on as a novice counselor in a drug and alcohol treatment clinic, I met a new male client, about 25 years, who was mandated to enter treatment as the result of getting a DUI. As is the usual procedure for assessing new clients, I asked him to tell me about his relationship with his mother, and in so many words he told me the following story.

He said his mother had been an alcoholic and had died about a year earlier. He said his parents had divorced when he was young, and that he had always lived with her in the same house. He said that her drinking had been bad for many years, and he described some of the heart-breaking ways he had cared for her on days when she was hungover and too sick to care for him, their roles being reversed. He said that one day she was taken to the ER when he was at work because a neighbor saw her having a seizure in the driveway and called 911.

He said she must have ran out of alcohol and was going to the store to get more when she fell. And through tears, he said that HE was the one who knew how to detox her, HE was the one who knew what medication to give her and how much, having lived through this many times with her, but the doctors wouldn't listen to him. She had never gained consciousness and he never had the chance to talk with her again because she died in cardiac arrest a few hours later.

And he went through that experience alone. And he had never told anyone else about it. And his drinking had gotten worse since that happened.

And when he was finished with his story, I remember that I didn't have to search for what to say to him. The words just came - "It sounds like you were a brave and good son to her, and that you tried your best. You were a remarkable gift to her, and you probably saved her many times. She very likely lived much longer because she had you, and I'll never forget what you did for her. I'm glad you survived and I'm glad we're here together today."

I became a better counselor that day.

Listening to people tell their stories, I saw first hand the courage it takes to reveal who we are. I was privileged to witness in them the positive results of sharing what had been locked away. I saw that once you do share your stories, the present begins to look different and things feel more settled. It's like taking the lid off of a pot that's been simmering unnoticed for a long time. The key is to keep sharing it until it's integrated into your own life story without the painful sting of remembrance, but instead providing another lesson in what it is to be a son, a daughter, wife, husband, friend to someone who is chronically ill.

I believe that most of what happens in life, even traumatic things, can be reasoned out and let go of with the wisdom we gain as evolving humans. But sometimes thing's that happen get buried deep in our minds, our muscles and our souls. "The body keeps the score," as Bessel Vanderkolk, a famous trauma therapist, says. Seeing that little boy on TV brought a story from the deepest part of my memory to the very surface of a new reality for me.

They linger, these stories, I have found, until they are told.

I believe that no matter how the stories come about in life, sharing them is proof of something I strongly believe. It's that the Universe has a power that wants us to connect with each other because we need love, we need healing and every once in a while we need to be a hero.

The Higher Power (HP)

Finding out how a spiritual relationship would work with a power greater than myself - the HP - took time. I needed to wrestle with it for a while the same way I wrestled with many recovery concepts.

I originally thought that living this "spiritual life" was about making daily attempts to stay on a narrow path of being a good person all the time, to be happy all the time, to be nice to everyone, etc. Of course, I would inevitably disappoint myself or someone else and things would go south somewhere along the line. Then I'd think I was getting this "God thing" wrong all over again, confounded by the poor results I had from my ever increasing efforts to do what I was sure God was expecting of me.

It was the frustration from failed attempts to "get it right" that slowly pushed me to see the limitations that my perfectionism was putting on my spiritual growth. I needed a new way forward where I could make mistakes and not feel so guilty or excluded by the judgmental God of my youth whom I was sure was keeping score of my transgressions.

Gratefully, I was to learn in time that the God of my youth was just me playing "mini-God" to myself, telling me what I thought I needed to do in order to stay on the straight and narrow. Most of the time the message was that I wasn't measuring up, and it had nothing to do with being loved by a benevolent being. When I accepted that this type of troubled thinking was of my own making, I knew that to keep growing spiritually, my concept of God going forward would have to be different. And from there, the way became clearer.

I saw that I didn't have to know exactly how living on a spiritual basis would work <u>before</u> I tried incorporating it into my daily life. I saw the folly in trying to be perfect so that things would work out, and I came to see the seeds of what a spiritual life really was - living from the inside out and not the outside in. It was connection of my intuition and the core of who I am to a force, a spark for good that I choose to call by many names - Higher Power, HP, God, or Good, or Universe, or Love, or Loving-Kindness, or He, or She. The name is only important for the moment I'm connecting to it. What really matters is that I have a relationship with that HP that I've built over time that's available to me 24/7,

- through the words and action of others that reach me and teach me
- through my intuitive thinking and gut awareness of how things really are
- through the softening of my heart that was hardened by a resentment
- through healing an old wound
- through being able to shift my focus from a problem to a solution
- through the help I get by helping someone else

The effects of this relationship have been radical in my life. The connection I'm able to make to such a power for help, for inspiration, for gratitude or for simple clarity is unique to each moment of the day. It might be,

- when I need to see things from 1,000 ft. above, or when I need to do a "close up" on the moment,
- when I need to wake up and see where love is in my life,
- when I need an old, traditional and safe patriarchal love for a sense of safety and protection, or
- when I can imagine what the care of a grandmother would feel like,
- when I feel my Mom coming through,
- when I need courage to do something that's difficult,
- when I need the strength to push through something that's overwhelming,
- when I get a surprise phone call from one of the kids,
- when I see the happy face of a newly sober person...
- It can be a million things.

It can be one thing.

But it's always there - that spark of promise and desire for a second chance, to continue, to try again; something I can't manufacture on my own; that I can't force feed myself.

It's opportunity that I didn't see coming.

It is hope.

I Hope

I hope for myself
at the end of my days
to feel my soul fulfilled
from years of adventure
and discovery of who I am,
leaving a long road behind and heading west
to my sanctuary by the sea,
my home on the shore
of blues and green, sand and sky,
to peace
in a place of beauty, wonder and ripeness
with someone interesting waiting for me
ready to listen to all I unpack, be it small or large
be it shocking or sane
all of it welcomed, fodder for long talks,
the talks, fodder for long silences
listening to the waves,
finally home, among my own
understood and accepted
with my people, my loves
and the flow of eternity,
the power that has always been with me,
palpable, pulsing
known to me firsthand at last

I

Identification

Once I was around recovery groups for a while, I began identifying more and more with the people I met. Even with those people I "wouldn't normally mix," as is often said in recovery circles, I could identify with their descriptions of cravings, triggers, and feelings, especially in those moments that came <u>before</u> picking up the first drink.

At the same time, however, and sometimes during the same meeting, I couldn't help but focus on the differences between my story and someone else's story. I was to learn in time that this tendency to <u>compare instead of relate</u> is common among people in recovery, and it was a talk I had with my friend one night after a meeting that made a huge difference in how I looked at my responsibility in recovery.

I shared with her that night how frustrated I was to have heard Larry, the speaker, talk about what seemed like every bottle of beer he drank in the Navy in WWII. In my arrogance, I went on to critique his talk, pointing out to her that his story was meandering and boring and that he was just an all-around poor speaker who should have asked for some help before he spoke in front of people.

Then Mary explained my "job" in AA. She said that all I was supposed to do when listening to someone's comment or story was to find <u>one thing</u> I could take away from it that would help me stay sober that day. Just <u>one thing.</u> So, having learned by then to follow her advice, I began applying

her suggestion and over time I saw the benefits of simplify-
ing the message to at least <u>one thing</u> I could take away from
the meeting. I also saw in stark relief just how judgmental I
was capable of being. The lesson I needed to truly connect
with this concept, however, was to come about year later at
the same meeting.

Once again, Larry was the speaker and he told his story
exactly the same way, from beginning to end. This time,
however, I actually heard what he was saying. When he
talked about the Navy this time, he said that at age 17
when he'd joined, it was the first time he'd been away from
his Iowa farming town. He said he was never so scared in
his life, heading for Europe on a giant military carrier at
sea. His first assignment was to take the overnight watch
on the top level in the pitch dark, and he said that the night
air was so black he could barely see his hand in front of
him. That's when he remembered that one of the keys he'd
been given to hold was to the room where they kept the
booze. He'd never drank before, but he knew what it could
do, so he opened the door, found the beer and drank away
the terror.

And I got it. I identified with the fear he described. I'd experienced a similar kind of fear at about the same age he did,
feeling I was in over my head with something and having no
help in sight. And I knew that same fear as an adult in my
early days of trying to stay sober - the fear of whether or not
I was going to make it through my day without a drink. That
kind of fear was overwhelming and fed my panic about what
to do next. To escape those feelings before recovery, I used
alcohol, just like Larry did. From Larry, and from many,

many people that I finally learned how to listen to, I was given another piece of the puzzle that helped me understand my own drinking, and it helped me want to continue digging in to my story - something I've always been intrigued with as you may be able to tell by this book.

As my recovery continued to progress, I was given another gift at a meeting one day when for the first time someone told me they'd identified with what I had shared. With her comment to me, I saw that the point of sharing at meetings was for others to be able to connect to that one thing that could help them through their day in sobriety.

I learned the importance of owning and sharing my stories about the dark days I lived through during my active addiction, especially acknowledging the harm I'd done to others. I saw that it gives someone else a chance to do the same and lighten the guilt and shame they carry from the confusing days of their own active addiction. How recovery works is that someday they'll have the chance to share it with someone else who is hurting from the shame and embarrassment of being addicted to alcohol and drugs, lightening that person's load, opening the door to who they are, and so on and so on.

I heard someone say in a meeting once that the reason we can name our mistakes is because someone else made them before us and named them. I loved that. It says that I didn't have to live alone in the remorse and regret of the mistakes I've made, living in the shadow of shame. It meant that I was just a human being like everyone else who makes mistakes. I fit into the human race.

Helping someone else identify the shame they may be carrying about the things they did during their active addiction is not easy. It usually requires telling one of my own embarrassing stories. It takes humbling myself. But my experience has been that once I share with someone else a shameful thing that I had once hidden away, it's as if more air is released from my painful memory.

I think that's a remarkable thing about recovery and I believe it's the HP at work, connecting the dots between people in ways I could never imagine. It's a happy mystery I'm in awe of.

I've learned in recovery that in order to have a sobriety that's worth keeping, I need to be a part of something greater than myself. Being a part of my group of friends in recovery is just that. With each other we have a unique quality of friendship that replaces the feelings of loneliness and being outside the herd, as they say. The chances I will identify with someone there are much greater than anywhere else because of what we have in common and the undeniable fact that no one got there on a winning streak - we all messed up somewhere with alcohol and drugs. It's when I compare myself to someone - their bottom, their consequences, parts of their story - that in effect I'm comparing my self out of the group. It's a sure way to return to that place in my mind where I never measure up and I don't fit it - a terrible place for a person in recovery to be.

In church basements, store fronts, buildings, and clubs where people in recovery meet, the loudest noise a person will hear as they walk in will not be the hushed tones and crying that could surely come from the sad stories there, but instead it will be laughter - the laughter that comes in the surprise of recognizing ourselves in each other; the laughter that comes in remembering the absurd ways we acted during our using days; the laughter that comes in that humble moment when we recognize the illogical and ridiculous ways we used to think we were right. And much more than that.

I believe that a lot of recovery is about getting back to the right size again - human size. My greatest wish is that by the end of my life, all of my stories are Anne size - stories that are without burden, that maybe helped another alcoholic mom let go of her shame. I hope that my load is lightened enough to fade away as on a cloud passing by. I think this Native American prayer from The Twelve Step Prayer Book (available on Prime) says it best:

"My Creator,
I seek strength not to be superior to my brothers and sisters, but to be able to fight my greatest enemy - myself. Make me ever ready to come to you with clean hands and straight eyes, so when life fades as a fading sunset my spirit may come to you without shame."

J

Just For Today

JUST FOR TODAY I will try to live through this day only, and not tackle all my problems at once. I can do something for twelve hours that would appall me if I felt that I had to keep it up for a lifetime.

JUST FOR TODAY I will be happy. This assumes to be true what Abraham Lincoln said, that "Most folks are as happy as they make up their minds to be."

JUST FOR TODAY I will adjust myself to what is, and not try to adjust everything to my own desires. I will take my "luck" as it comes, and fit myself to it.

JUST FOR TODAY I will try to strengthen my mind. I will study. I will lean something useful. I will not be a mental loafer. I will read something that requires effort, thought and concentration.

JUST FOR TODAY I will exercise my soul in three ways: I will do somebody a good turn, and not get found out; if anybody knows of it, it will not count. I will do at least two things I don't want to do - just for exercise. I will not show anyone that my feelings are hurt; they may be hurt, but today I will not show it.

JUST FOR TODAY I will be agreeable. I will look as well as I can, dress becomingly, keep my voice low, be courteous, criticize not one bit. I won't find fault with anything, nor try to improve or regulate anybody but myself.

JUST FOR TODAY I will have a program. I may not follow it exactly but I will have it. I will save myself from two pests: hurry and indecision.

JUST FOR TODAY I will have a quiet half hour all by myself and relax. During this half hour, sometime, I will try to get a better perspective on my life.

JUST FOR TODAY I will be unafraid. Especially I will not be afraid to enjoy what is beautiful, and to believe that as I give to the world, so the world will give to me.

Printed from https://al-anon.org of the public domain

K

Kindness

I remember my Mom taking me along with her several times as a little kid to deliver gallons of water to a friend of hers - a mother with children, not far from our house. My mom took the water from our tap in gallon jugs to this woman because she had none, my Mom said. Of course, now I realize that her water had been shut off, likely because of past due water bills. That's who my Mom was. She knew about the fear that goes with hardship and living without.

There was more to that woman's story that I was too young to grasp at the time, but I like to imagine that she and my Mom were good friends, and they shared a confidence about the kind of troubles that might lead to such a crisis - enough so that my Mother was the one she called for help. The kind of shame and embarrassment that might come from not having enough water to run a household is not something easily shared, I'm sure. And the kind of shame and embarrassment about the family issues that could bring you to such a calamity wouldn't be easy to share either. I know my Mom helped her shoulder some of those burdens during that time and I can imagine the relief she gave this woman with the simple gift of water. In that memory, I can see the power of love and friendship in hard times.

Those were tough terms that woman was living by. I knew that, even as a small child, and I will never forget the kindness of my Mother towards that poor soul. She was lucky to have you, Mom, and so was I.

L

Letting Go

"I knew what to do. I just hadn't let go yet."
From, "Heard At Coffee With Friends"

I like getting to the bottom of things. I like drilling down and being able to see all the angles of a situation. It's a part of my creative side that sees and hears my world in ways that are uniquely mine, and I've come to see it as a good thing about who I am. I've also come to see, however, that drilling down doesn't always work for everything - especially problem solving. It's true that I may see things for what they are a bit clearer, but past a certain point it turns into over-thinking and can make the problem seem bigger, catching me in a stressful loop of yet another vain attempt at finding a solution.

Sometimes the answer is just to let go of everything - right there on the spot - to drop my hands to my sides, stop digging and let myself <u>be</u> - focusing only on my breathing and returning to it if the hamster wheel in my head starts up again. I do that until I'm calm enough to move forward once more.

Another letting go tool I like to use is a visualization of myself standing on the edge of a cliff - arms out like wings, toes to the edge, looking up to the sky, taking a big breath and finally pushing off - flying just for the pure beauty of flying. Just being, with no need for control. Weightless. It is relief. It is peace. And often, just a few minutes of this kind of self care is all I need to return to myself and the wisdom I have to know the next right move to make.

If I can let go in the moment, I can reach the calm of knowing that everything is ok right now and that I'll be ok because I'm sober and know how to handle life on life's terms. Then the courage I already have comes alive again and gives me the personal power I need to keep letting go. The choices I make from there are mine as a reasonable, thinking person. Decisions don't have to be the impulsive reactions that once ruled my life. Whatever the case may be, I have come to believe in and to respect the power of letting go. I think the following poems say it well.

Flight

I wasn't standing on a cliff
or perched on a branch.
I wasn't posed on a diving board
waiting for the courage to push off.
I was simply brave enough to close my eyes one morning
alone, sitting on a bench
along a sunny footpath In Carpinteria,
joined by a light breeze
making it's way up from the seashore,
swirling with the tide as it rose
in this safe place for all creatures
where white Ibis gathered
and mountains sloped to the water,
all purple canyons and crevices,

exposing the good old earth in all it's glory,
holding my mind and spirit in that moment
as in a deep cleft
when suddenly I was pulled upward, back arched, arms out
beckoned to unfurl my wings
feeling my heart open
by virtue, by grace, by a miracle
as the sea air gave just enough draft
to set me in flight to join the white winged calliope,
circling the cove
sounding out
"Begin again, my dear."
"Continue"

Lighthouse

For Elizabeth
I wasn't fearless yet
when I was doing those things,
staying just within the bounds of what was acceptable,
corralled mostly by guilt.

Something GOT me fearless, though,
changed me and
woke me up to my own power.

I think it was the alcohol and drugs,
and not because they actually helped me to see the light
and follow my dreams.

No.
It was because they were dead weights around my neck,
slowly drowning me
just below the surface of my murky past
until in one fearless moment,
I broke for the surface,

Not just to survive,
but to live the wild life I always wanted
betraying my willful, cynical self,

With every breath, every lesson and loss,
braver,
the fear falling away like scales from my eyes,
sometimes quickly,
sometimes slowly,

To find myself in time,
suited up and ready for the high dive,
the high note,
the high road,

And learning to keep the high watch from my lighthouse
for that rascal Fear to show it's ugly mug again
like it tried to do today,
unbidden and unwelcome,
with it's stormy seas, danger and drama,
until I let it go back to the rough waters it came from,
to watch it miraculously calmed once again
by Experience, by Wisdom,
feeling myself once again whole, courage in tact.

The Long View

Years ago I was a drug and alcohol counselor in an evening intensive outpatient treatment program in a suburb of Cleveland, OH. People who attended the program committed to completing eight weeks of group and individual therapy, and it could be intense, just as the name suggests.

To witness people as they incorporate changes into their daily lives without drugs and alcohol was a gift to me. I was constantly impressed by their willingness to share how they were handling the ups and downs of early recovery - no small feat. My job was to provide the therapy that would guide them through those times and offer a safe place to talk with others going through the same changes. What happened in one group session has stayed with me all these years and is a great example of the serendipitous moments that can shift how you see things - right then and there. But first, a little background.

I'd just started working at this particular treatment center which was on the 7th floor of a high rise building on the east side of town. I was getting used to my new office one evening, working alone, when I was amazed by what I saw through the large west-facing window I was lucky to have there. On the bottom edge of the enormous, bright yellow sun that was setting on the horizon, I could clearly see a calm Lake Erie, about 25 miles away, its water flickering iridescent greens and yellows and a boat the color of bright gold, reflected from the sun, as it was moving across the water... and it was stunning.

A few nights later during a group session of 8 people that I was facilitating, several shared about the difficulties they were having with serious family issues and the complications of re-entry into the workplace that can happen as a clean and sober person. As the session went on, the group dynamic built to one particular moment when feelings were raw with sadness and frustration; where they'd become stuck in their problems with few solutions under their belts yet - a common place to be in early recovery. And then I remembered the sunset.

To pivot from the negativity that had fallen over the group, I asked them to follow me down the hall to my office, knowing that the sun was just setting. Once outside my door, I opened it for them to enter and simply said, "Look," and they all gravitated to the window with a view of Lake Erie, ablaze and shimmering in the distance. After a few quick "ooo"s and "wow"s, they were silent, standing still, taking in the moment together. They stayed there for quite a few minutes, each returning to the group room when they were ready. I began the session again when everyone was back.

The take away from that experience for them was realizing that they actually possessed the ability to shift their focus from the pain that had just been so palpable in group to the beauty of a sunset and the possibilities that a different perspective could hold - sometimes quickly and radically. As I liked to do at the end of a meaningful group like that, we wrote a poem together, and I watched once again as people who were once strangers came together and formed into their own unique support group. The poem, as I remember, was about change - sometimes found in the most surprising places, when you least expect it, in a group of people who once felt lost and now were found, in a sunset on a far away lake, taking in the long view from 7 floors up.

Loving Kindness

There is a Buddhist concept called "loving kindness" that means to fully give of yourself in compassion and love with an awareness and appreciation of the natural world,* and it's a virtue I try to cultivate in my life. I love the link of those two words - <u>love</u> which I feel intuitively from the core of who I am, and <u>kindness</u> that I can show to others in thought, word and deed.

Luckily, I've been the receiver of many acts of loving-kindness in my life from the good people I've had around me, but I know there are times I've missed a gesture or a kind word from someone, only to realize later just what it was they'd been trying to convey. I've learned that it's only my expectations about what I <u>think</u> love is supposed to look and feel like that can get in the way of seeing the love that's right in front of me.

Like many of us, I grew up thinking that love was some romantic version of what I saw in the movies or read about in books and magazines. Fantasies of finding true love filled my head as a girl, and it took time and some hard knocks to learn that those images are distortions of what love really is. Today I know love to be:

- Cleaning the house
- Fixing the faucet
- Making a meal

- Doing the dishes
- Doing the laundry
- Take out the trash
- Putting gas in the car
- Remembering birthdays and anniversaries
- Sending cards in the mail
- Remembering someone's name you just met
- Calling someone to look outside at the rainbow
- Going to the store for someone who can't get out of the house
- Checking up on a sick neighbor
- Bringing flowers when someone dies
- Sending an email to an old friend just to say hi
- Taking a trip to see someone you miss
- Giving encouragement to someone going through a hard time
- Growing a garden
- etc., etc

And I love that all of these are acts can be done with or without saying a word, in the least romantic scene, without fanfare, during the course of any day. If you note the time and effort someone puts into giving of themselves - you can hear it, loud and beautifully clear - from their heart to yours.

* The Wise Heart, A Guide to the Universal Teachings of Buddhist Psychology, by Jack Kornfield, 2008, Bantam Books, a division of Random House, Inc., New York.

M

Meditation

"Go With The Flow"

I love that saying. It fits beautifully into a meditation practice I use about water. I imagine I'm in a canoe on a lazy river, not paddling, letting the current take me along, moving under the shade of tall tree tops, with sunlight breaking through in random patterns, sometimes as sparkling diamonds that dot the water here and there. It's wonderfully calming, and I've used this meditation enough to have a sense of when I'm going <u>against</u> the river - paddling furiously, anxiously troubled about what may be ahead or about what I may have just left behind.

What I've learned from this meditation is that in times of trouble, I need to detach from whatever has gotten me in an emotional twist and return to the river, getting back in the canoe and beginning again from wherever I am, moving letting the current move me along. If I let myself go with the flow, I've come to trust that the river will always guide me through whatever lies ahead.

I think "the flow" is what people in recovery call "life on life's terms," or that part of being alive that I have no control over, which is mostly all of it - life's terms - not mine. My attitude and my reactions - everything that I am responsible for - are pretty much the only things I can control, and even those are iffy at times. My attitude towards life for a long time was "I know there's some kind of problem in here somewhere, so let's get to it" - not the easier, softer way to live, to be sure.

I had to learn that if I don't look at everything as though it's a race or a competition I have to win, I can get through the rough currents with peace of mind when I put my head on my pillow at day's end. Trying to determine an outcome just keeps me trapped in whirlpools of circular thinking about things I can't control. The stress and anxiety that come with control can also wear a person down - body, mind and spirit - sometimes terribly, with negative consequences for the autoimmune system, gastro system, nervous system and cognitive functioning. In the end, life's too short to keep going against what is.

Today, if I'm in the midst of the pain and turmoil that can result from trying to hold onto a person, place or thing that's not mine, I've come to find that something remark-able can happen - something that's made a huge change in my emotional balance and well being. My meditation prac-tice "pays it forward" right in that moment of struggle and turmoil with the keen awareness of the anxiety I'm feeling right then, and after a simple and immediate acknowledge-ment of it, I can suddenly see where I'm getting in my own way and making things much harder than they have to be. If I can stop fighting everything and everyone and pull the paddles into the boat at that moment, the way forward becomes much more manageable and even enjoyable. The power of meditation is remarkable indeed for the person I am who at one time could be lost in the intensity of anxiety and on-going recreation of troubles in my mind.

Because I practice the self-care of meditation and visualization, I know how to shift my thinking from negative to positive. Sometimes the message I receive is to set a boundary, or make a decision about something, or let go of something, or just plain relax for a bit. I've come to trust this process, and because of it, staying with the current is no longer the challenge it once was. Today I can go with the flow.

My Bravery

The bravest thing I ever did,
braver than giving birth to my boys,
or marrying for a second time
or moving across the country
or asking for a raise I knew I was worth but not likely to get
or starting my own practice
or helping to start a treatment center for women
or retiring -
braver than any of that
was to break away from the fears that bound me to my
family home, and leave.

I was reminded of true bravery when I recently saw a news
story on TV about a little girl, maybe 7 years old, who lived
in Syria. She was being interviewed by a reporter while the
bombs of their uncivil war were being dropped in the distance, loud enough to be heard at times from where she
and the journalist were seated. Even though apparently safe
in that moment, she was obviously nervous, shifting back
and forth as she answered questions about what daily life
was like for her while it was being destroyed around her. The
crumbed wall behind them was evidence of the on-going
destruction.

I watched as the uncomfortable interview continued, only to
be shocked when in certain moments the little girl suddenly

stopped talking so she could listen to the sound that each bomb made when it exploded. She would then announce the technical name of the bomb with a blank expression on her face, a skill someone likely taught her as a way to have even the most minute control over what was out of her control. Her sweet face was so tired and care-worn, her little body so thin and tense. It was heartbreaking to watch and I'll never forget it.

I'll never forget her because I can't. I know the fear of captivity and the unpredictable nature of conflict - certainly not on that scale, not even close - but I know the seed of it, planted in my childhood.

I'm aware of the panic a child can experience that comes from realizing that the adults don't know what to do anymore, when there is real danger that may show up that day, and when you need to know the safest place to hide or whether to fight back, especially when you're a little older and tired of the helplessness. Then you want to fight back.

Yes, the bravest thing I ever did was to leave the conflicts raging in the life of my family. Finding a way to get out of it took me down some dark roads that are part of my story, but before that journey began, I had to leave the only home I'd known. I did it by realizing that I simply didn't have a dog in that fight anymore, and if I stayed, I would only be contributing to a losing battle.

After I'd been gone for a while, I learned that there are other skirmishes in the world that require bravery. And because I'd been a hero for myself, I knew what one looked like. It can be a young woman who says enough is enough, or it can be a small beauty from Syria, creating a sense of safety for herself in an unsafe home, having learned the unpredictability of war and the need to be ready to run. I prayed then and now that she may find peace someday, that dear, brave child.

Marriage

Asserted,
an essay

Everyone makes mistakes. Everyone hurts someone they love, and everyone gets hurt by someone they love in ways big and small. It's only human to mess up now and then. Knowing this, however, doesn't help much during those times when it feels like everyone else knows the embarrassing thing you did. The criticism and judgment of others that may follow (whether real or imagined), can still call The Committee to order for another round of shame and self incrimination, and it can make the day (the week? the months?) miserable.

Offering restitution can hopefully amend the situation, but without genuine resolution, people can become frozen by the intense reactions they have to what occurred - both offender and the offended. They can't (or refuse to) see a way out of the conflict. When that happens in a committed relationship, it can be the source of on-going and some-times very serious consequences, with over-the-top defense mechanisms creating a no win situation that repeats and repeats.

I once walked with a good friend through a particularly hard time in their marriage - where the road was paved with resentments and conflicts that had never been resolved, and their faults and flaws were there for others to see. It was painful to watch. I hated seeing my friend in such fear, believing their marriage might be over. And it was also painful because I, too, had walked a similar path in my marriage. As I went through the darkness of my friend's troubled times, I couldn't help but remember the darkness that once permeated throughout my own troubled times.

Gratefully during those days with my friend, I was also reminded of the turning point I had reached one day years earlier when I realized how long it had been since I did anything meaningful for myself. I knew in a moment of clarity that if I didn't start meeting my own needs and goals, apart from my husband's, I would lose myself once again and perhaps never find out who I was or what I wanted to do with the rest of my life. From a time of desperation came empowerment and the way forward was suddenly clearer. I started living in solutions without such a keen focus on what the problem was.

Whenever a problem is exposed in a relationship, I believe we get a choice of whether to use the guts of it for the good it holds - for growth and clarity of the road ahead - or to put our heads back in the sand, only to continue struggling for air through the limitations of pridefulness, stubbornness and denial. In my own marriage, it's been the willingness to get the help we needed that made the difference between staying stuck in the conflict or finding a way forward where our faults and flaws - the guts of it - could be sorted out and used to understand each other better.

With that work, I began to see marriage as a two-way street, and on my side, I had to set new boundaries, with less people pleasing, more assertiveness and less willingness to live with peace at any cost. The cost was already too high. If I wanted change, I had to assert who I was as an equal partner. It was vital to my mental health and happiness - to my very soul.

I've gotten to know my side of the street very well over the years, and it took time, but I learned that I didn't have to know everything about my husband's side to be ok with mine. Of course, I'm interested in what's happening on his side and I enjoy the times he wants to share it with me. I enjoy sharing my side with him as well. The point of these delineations is to maintain clear communication lines that have become necessary for us to add to the foundation we already have, with each of us bringing our own input and feedback to it. That approach is very important to me and continues as the key to being able to work together as a couple in recovery.

Eventually, my friend's marriage took a turn for the better and they returned to each other across the field that had once divided them, exposing the fault lines to be wary of, the rabbit holes to avoid, but also the great expanse that holds their future. It's been a gift to behold and something I wish for everyone going through a hard time in their relationships, especially if the shame of unwanted scrutiny from others has been a part of it. And in regard to that kind of shame, I reached a point in my interactions with other people that can be explained very well by a statement I once heard. It's that, if the people around me don't get me, they're not my people. It's that simple.

Today, I stick with people who get me. They're my teachers. They taught me to assert myself, how to be a better listener (and be a little deaf sometimes), and how to see beyond the faults we all have. Most importantly, I've learned that the troubled times I've lived through don't have to define me or my relationships. They're lessons if I choose to look at them that way. Thankfully, most of the time I see them that way, and when I do, I continue to grow in the knowledge of who I am. That's the best way I know of making the relationship I have with my husband stronger, interesting, fun and worth keeping. It makes me a better friend to others, too, and for all of that, I could never be grateful enough.

N

New York on 9/11/20

"The city, for the first time in its long history, is destructible. A single flight of planes no bigger than a wedge of geese can quickly end this island fantasy, burn the towers, crumble the bridges, turn the underground passages into lethal chambers, cremate the millions. The intimation of mortality is part of New York now; in the sounds of jets overhead, in the black headlines of the latest editions. All dwellers in cities must live with the stubborn fact of annihilation; in New York the fact is somewhat more concentrated because of the concentration of the city itself, and because, of all targets, New York has a certain clear priority. In the mind of whatever perverted dreamer might loose the lightning, New York must hold a steady, irresistible charm."

From This is New York, by E.B. White, The Little Book Room, Publishers, Ny, NY 1949

As a young adult, I was sure that New York City was the place for me. It held a crazy hope that a dreamer like me needed in order to make it in the world as an artist. I wanted to sing for a living, and I wanted to continue on the road I'd begun at age 20 in Cleveland. I'd heard that you either had to go to L.A. or New York to make it as a performer, and since I'd always loved what New York represented - the new Americans, the scrappers who knew how to use a second chance - choosing New York as the first destination in my plan for success was easy.

Because of the way my future evolved, however, such a bold move would not be for me. I never had the proper training, the resume, the resources, the seed money, the connections - all sounding like excuses as I write this, I suppose, and maybe they are to a degree, but from my experience back then I knew the competitiveness that can exist for performers in the music business, having been one in the small arena of Cleveland, and it could be daunting.

Given an honest and realistic evaluation of what it would take to make a start at such an endeavor, I can see that what I truly lacked to pull it off was courage. Bravado I had, and that may have gotten me so far, but I was also very susceptible to criticism and lack of belief in myself. Those things plagued me.

I continued to play it small right where I was, and slowly over time, gave away the dream, piece by piece, until where I landed held nothing of my performing self. I turned the fire I once had for singing against myself instead, burning my insides with regret in moments when I remembered what I gave up, tamped down by alcohol, drugs, relationships, work, then a house, children, moving...

Reading E.B. White, I remember being surprised to find that he considered New York to be vulnerable, to be "destructible," way back in 1949. He knew that by being out there on the map - with towers, bridges and subways - New York became a target for those forces of evil and nuclear power that had been unleashed on the world by then.

Today, I find myself wishing I'd put myself out there like the City of New York itself continues to do - all grit and muscle with a shine on the talent it takes to remain viable despite great losses. I wish I'd stuck it out, finding my way, believing in myself. I might have failed here and there; might have been hurt mercilessly. But if I'd been able to survive such trials with my dignity and some momentum in tact, I'd have survived like the powerhouse that New York City is, and I believe I might have done all right. I'll never really know.

So, once again I'm left to say good night, New York, on this sad day of all sad days and to marvel at your survival. I'm saying good night with gratitude for the daydreams of you I've carried all these years. They're a part of what made me the person I am today, helping me find other ways to make music, with other dreamers. And I'm saying good night with the hope of being alive for many more days to come, to be vital, with more chances to be uniquely me, just like I hope for you, New York. I hope. Good, good night.

O

One Day at a Time

"You can't work on everything at once."
From, "Heard at Coffee With Friends"

He said, "Write it on your heart that every day is the best day in the year. He is rich who owns the day, and no one owns the day who allows it to be invaded with fret and anxiety. Finish every day and be done with it. You have done what you could. Some blunders and absurdities, no doubt, crept in. Forget them as soon as you can, tomorrow is a new day; begin it well and serenely, with too high a spirit to be cumbered with your old nonsense. This new day is too dear, with its hopes and invitations to waste a moment on yesterdays."

Ralph Waldo Emerson, From Collected Poems and Translations, H. Bloom and P. Kane, Editors, originally published in 1867

Overage

My friend Sarah once said that alcoholics and addicts were "over-feelers," and I grasped that idea the minute I heard it. I've been a kind of "over-feeler" my whole life. I just seem to be on a different frequency than a lot of people. And being 70 years old with a lot of self-reflection and recovery, I also think I was born that way. It's just part of who I am. And the cool thing is, I like that about me. I feel things deeply. I believe deeply. I love deeply. I have deep concerns, deep desires and wishes. Regardless, I still like that about me.

I like experiencing life to the fullest. I like being caught off guard with gratitude for a beautiful Florida sky. I like that I have a BS detector, too, and I like knowing that I will always look out for myself and those that I love - especially my children. They're in a category where it's hard for me not to be on "over," I have to admit. I just have so much love for them that the "overage" is just there naturally. I can't help it.

When I'm aware that someone may not get me or like me, I'm ok with that today. Life's too short to be around people who don't understand how I feel about things and how I "do life." Don't get me wrong. I know I'm not perfect and I still need honest feedback from trusted people, but someone telling me to be different or feel differently than what I am (with, "Calm down!" or "Stop worrying!") doesn't work for me. I turning myself inside out emotionally to please other people for too long. Not anymore.

○

I like being "right sized" for the life I lead and the situations I find myself in. It takes humility for that to happen, and I've eaten some humble pie to get there, for sure. It's all good and it's all a part of my story. So far, so good, I'd say.

$\mathcal{P}$

Pain

One of the topics I used in group therapy with clients was pain. I usually started the discussion by writing the word PAIN on the white board and asked them to share their thoughts about it regardless of whether it was emotional or physical pain. It didn't matter. Of all the groups I facilitated over the years, this topic brought the most consistent responses. Some of them were:

- I'm afraid it won't stop.
- Feeling pain makes me mad.
- I want to change it to something funny
        happy
        different, etc.
- If someone else is in pain, I try to fix it for them.
- I want to stop it any way I can.
- I pretend it's not happening.
- No one wants to be around me when I'm in pain.
- I hide it. I won't let anyone see me in pain.
- I thought it would kill me.

Then at some point I'd usually ask what good can come from pain, what lessons, and again, very similar answers came over the years:

- I found out who my friends were when I lost my marriage

    mom

    dad

    job, etc.

- I didn't think I'd be able to handle it, but I did.

- I didn't know Tylenol worked - I always thought I needed opiates.

- I'm learning I can live with the loss.

- I don't like it, but I can live with it.

- Everyone feels pain sometimes.

- You can't avoid it.

Watching people begin to trust the process of recovery and share about the very thing that brought them there - pain - is a very rewarding thing, indeed. I count it among my greatest experiences in life and will be forever grateful for having the privilege of seeing people acknowledge the pain they've experienced and reach out from it for help. It is the human spirit to survive on display and it awakened my spirit day after day for many years. I also got to witness the courage of fellow counselors who leaned into the pain of others, sitting by their side, listening. They did it because they had suffered, too, and they already knew it wouldn't kill them. They knew how to bring relief to a person who was wounded on the inside. It was their calling. And it was pure gift to watch. Thanks everyone. Thanks, Universe.

Parenting

I think the hardest thing about parenting is knowing what your kids are supposed to learn on their own and when you're supposed to show them. The following poems tell the story of how I got a glimpse into that confounding question.

Waving

One morning in early winter many years ago
when the kids were in school
I took our two little Cairn terriers
to a park near our house for a walk.

Combining their excitement
with a slippery trail
and my distracted thoughts as a worried mother that day,
I became tangled in their leashes
and with one quick pull ended up flat on my back
in the snow that had fallen the night before.

Surprised and thankfully unhurt,
I felt something come over me,
holding me where I was on the ground
instead of getting up right away
and back on the trail.

A My Life... According to the Alphabet

I just stayed there
with no one else around
but Buddy and Duffy, my furry loves,
patiently sitting by my side
waiting for my next move.

And in the stillness of that moment
I looked up at the large maple tree in front of me,
still holding its late fall leaves of red,
filtering a blue sky from the background.

Then came my next surprise.

I watched as one leaf started waving and flapping.

In the whole tree nothing else moved,
just that one wild leaf,
and as I laid there watching it dance,
the beauty of an insight so clear
from deep within my gut
came to me,
telling me that the worries I was carrying that day -
the worries that brought me down to the ground
about my boy
and my feeble attempts to change him -
could be explained in one waving leaf,
showing me that to stand out
on his own,
different from the rest
and apart from me,

P

was what he had been trying to do all along.
That's what this chapter in our lives had been all about.

And the choices that laid ahead of him
were his to make, not mine.
My new role was to watch as things unfolded for him,
and to be there to help when he needed it,
seeing that the pathway to peace of mind for myself
was going to lay in the acceptance of those limitations.
For that moment, I didn't need to know anything more.

And for the first time that morning, my heart and my mind
were at peace.

Then suddenly feeling the cold seep into my bones,
I pulled myself up,
shook off the snow
and my little dogs guided me along
excited for whatever was around the next turn.

The Wide World Yet To Be

Our son was far from home in his late teens.
preparing himself for a future in the wide world yet to be.
his father and I knowing by then that
he needed others to show him how things worked in the
world.

Once, at the end of a weekend family visit
we dropped him off at his house
where I said my best good-bye in the front hall
with a stiff upper lip.

then quickly turning to make my exit without tears.
I came upon the most unexpected sight -
an amazing array of the shoes of teenage boys.
toes touching toes, some upside down or heel-to-toe
sharing the same wall by the front door
ready to spring into action
hopeful
ready for anything
come what may

Peace of Mind

"I walked over and looked closer at the status of the goddess. She was wearing a headdress with a skull and a cobra and a crescent moon. Maybe this is what peace of mind was all about: having a poisonous snake on your head and smiling anyway."

Wally Lamb, "I Know This Much is True", from goodreads. com, "Quotes" by Wally Lamb.

Yes. Exactly.
Poisonous snakes.
Crescent moons.
Skulls.
Even on my head.
And I say, so what?
Take my picture!

People Pleasing

My friend, Caleb, used to say that whatever other people think is none of my business. That includes what other people think about me. If someone doesn't like me, that's ok because it's none of my business. Oh, it may sting a bit - especially if someone is a "biter." Some people bite, I have found, with a snarky comment or put down that comes out of left field. That can be rough to experience, for sure, but I've learned that it's not imperative that everybody likes me. Sometimes I don't like them either. That's ok, too. If you like everybody, a friend said to me, then you're not hanging around enough people!

The impact that other people have on my life is ultimately up to me. My goal is to be comfortable in my own skin with no emotional hangovers to clean up at the end of the day, able to put my head on my pillow at peace with myself. I paid a lot in stress and worry to gain that perspective, and it's one I intend to keep gaining from in the days ahead.

Perfectionism

Along I-25 in Wyoming you can still see remnants of the Oregon Trail where early pioneers followed each other in wagon trains from the eastern U.S. to start new lives in the West in the early 1800s. In certain sections, you can see the ruts that thousands of stage coach and wagon wheels formed, the deep furrows as hard as cement. If you've ever tried getting out of a rut like that on a bike trail or in icy snow when you're driving, you know how hard it can be. I think that trying to be perfect is a lot like that, too. The over planning, over preparation, high expectations and clinging to worn out ideas of how things should be can make it impossible to live life as it actually is.

Demanding that unrealistic standards be met can be a compulsion and preoccupation that rivals the difficulties of chemical addiction. The constant vigilance required to have things turn out one way and not another can trap a person in a repetitive, predictable equation of how things will often work out - something like this:

The need to control outcomes = pressure to get it right = over-planning, over doing = high expectations which eventually can't be met = disappointment = fears of being a failure and what others will think = trying harder to get it right the next time = more over-planning, over-doing, pressure = more unrealistic expectations = eventual disappointment = fears of what other people think = trying harder, etc....and on and on it goes.

You can insert alcohol and/or drugs anywhere in the equation. Like a "friend" who lies to us, it says that you can escape the growing panic and desperation that comes with the repeated attempts to control people, places and things. All you need is a drink or a drug. The "ism" of perfectionism includes the same distorted mix of thoughts, feelings and behaviors that come with the "ism" in alcoholism or any kind of addiction.

Like all of the "isms," perfectionism prevents a person from learning how to come to terms with the uncertainties that life can present. I know from long personal experience the toll that needing people, places and things to look a certain way can take on a person. The same mental, spiritual and physical problems that are linked to codependency can able be linked to perfectionism. They go hand-in-hand. And it can be exhausting.

Over time, I found that having peace of mind at the end of the day outweighs any need I have for things to work out the way I want them to. That means that I still need a "to do" list and a plan to get certain things done because that's part of life. But I've also learned to set aside my expectations of exactly <u>how</u> those things will get done. I don't have that kind of power. When I leave those details up to HP, I can see the ruts up ahead, and today, I can take a different way.

Prayer

I think that connection with God works the way I heard it explained years ago: prayer is talking to God and meditation is listening to God. That rang true for me then and still does today. And while my conception of God has evolved in many ways over the years, the idea that I can simply put my thoughts out to the Universe is still comforting. I don't know exactly what's happening when I talk with/at/to the HP, but I feel better when I do. I think it's like opening a channel from my head to my heart. Somehow it puts me in sync with myself and the world around me.

One way I still pray today was suggested to me years ago. It's to say a prayer of gratitude according to the alphabet. Along those lines, this book is a prayer, the seeds of which follow:

A - me, Anne

B - my boys

C - Colorado

D - my dogs

E - eating!

F - family, friends

G - Group Of Drunks

H - The HP

I - Ice cream

J - Jeff

K - my kids

L - love in my life

M - music

N - nighttime

O - the ocean

P - pansies

Q - quiet

R - recovery, rest

S - sunrise, sunset

T - time, tears

U - the Universe

V - my vacuum cleaner

W - water

X - x-rays

Y - YOU

Z - the zoo

...just to name some of them...

Q

In Quarantine

by Kim Stafford, poet laureate of The State of
Oregon, 2018-2020,
Copied from the website, <u>The Writer's Almanac
With Garrison Keillor</u>

"After they furnished us mortality estimates
on a sheet to post in the hall, after they sealed
the doors, after they counted our days of water—
by megaphone from outside the perimeter—after
they locked the gate, and then drove away, after our
desperate questions had exhausted all our tears, after we
looked at each other, first with suspicion of contagion,
then with curiosity, and then with love, someone
found a guitar, remembered a song, and we all
got in a line, laughing arm in arm, and danced."

"In Quarantine" reminded me of the wonder and power of
a good poem. Kim's words took me right back to being on
lock-down with my husband during the pandemic years. It
was harrowing at first, especially for the impact it was having
on our children and their busy lives far away from where we
lived, but eventually my husband and I found a groove allow-
ing us to return to being the good cooks we had been, the
good exercisers we had once been, the lovers of good music
we are, and the good friends we once were in our beginning
days together, when what mattered most was getting to know
each other, with curiosity and love. That was the best part.

R

Rejection

If I happen to be overly sensitive during the day with feelings of rejection, I like to use one of the following reminders to get back on track. Some of them I've picked up from the wisdom of other people, some I've learned from my own hard knocks. They all give me the boost I need from time to time, and I'm grateful for each one.

Everyone doesn't secretly hate you.

Everyone doesn't know you, and everyone is mostly thinking about themselves. Besides, there are two kinds of business: my business and none of my business. What other people think about you is none of your business. Quit giving them free rent in your head.

You don't have to be perfect to be loved.

Besides, you can't be perfect. No one can. There is no "perfect" anything. Screw perfection.

Making mistakes doesn't make you a bad person.

They make you human. Even big mistakes. They're lessons - not testaments to all the mistakes you've ever made in your life. That's just guilt, and screw guilt, too.

Your intrusive thoughts are lying to you.

If you notice that you have repeating negative thoughts, click a "pause" button in your mind, stop what you're doing and find a place to be comfortably alone for a few minutes. Begin by breathing in steady, full breaths followed by steady, full exhales. With eyes closed, envision the thoughts as if they're going round and round in a circle. You don't have to see the words perfectly. Just know that they're there, circling round and round. Then imagine that at one point in the circle it breaks open and sends the thoughts out in a line, floating up and away from you. Sense their release, keep breathing, and repeat this until you're calm again, open your eyes and then go do the next right thing for yourself or someone else. With practices, you'll get better at stopping the saboteur in your committee. Learning to pause is a simple but powerful tool for managing the moments of self-destruction that can catch us off guard.

<u>The people in your life want to be there.</u>

Take them at face value until you know differently. You might be judging their motives because of something from your past, so be aware of the rabbit holes that fear of rejection can take you down. If you can't shake the feeling that they're going to leave, ask them about it. If they care about you, they'll listen and talk it through with you. How to move forward from there will become clearer after that. It will help you decide for yourself what's good for you and what's not. It's up to you.

Retirement

written at the beach

Now It's Christmas

The size of our Christmas celebrations has been shrinking since our last couple of moves, and this year was the smallest it's ever been. We've down-sized so much that we even bought a skinny tree that somehow comes together only if you use enough lights and ornaments - a little like Charlie Brown's.

This year I gave away another box of decorations to Goodwill, an act of surrender to the reality of living in a smaller house than we used to. "I just don't have the room anymore," I kept telling myself as I boxed up each ornament, each snowman, and each wreath, hoping a sweet young Mom somewhere had the room, and would take them to her home as she tried to make Christmas happen for her kids like I did for mine.

This year it didn't take long to get our house back to normal when all was said and done. The decorations were easily packed away after New Year's Day, even the extra storage box I've learned to keep around every year for the stragglers - the wreath I forgot on the front door, the picture on the hallway table, the candles on the buffet.

So, with another holiday under my belt I returned to my desk and the morning writing routine I'd put off during the holidays. And as I eased myself into the familiar setting around me, I was surprised to see that a Christmas song, "Joy," by George Winston, was still in the music queue on my computer, one I hadn't heard during the season. I clicked "play" and sat back in my chair, entranced by the rich sound, forgetting all about what I had planned to do.

Then I closed my eyes, took some deep breaths and was taken away in my mind to our home on the lake, many years ago when the kids were little, opening their presents, fire in the fireplace, music on the stereo...

And a beautiful feeling of security swept over me, washing me with gratitude for my husband and the chance we had to make Christmas memories for our boys, the warmth of them holding me as if I was there again, watching the snow fall in the yard, assured it was all worth it.

"Now, it's Christmas," I whispered, and I stayed in that place for a while, letting more music play, touched by sweet memories of family and friends. And when my daydreaming was done, I drifted back to my desk and the tasks I'd set for myself that day, thankful for the priceless gift of contentment I'd been given, reminding me of the power for good that exists in the world, leaving me in awe once again to marvel at my good fortune.

Dredging

The dredger is in the river today,
cutting out the beds of weeds and
clearing out the muck that's filled it

since the last time they did it
to deepen the route for the boats
that are bejeweled and bedecked
with vacationers and fishing charters -
the floating participants in the never ending parade
on this well-used outlet to the sea.

Seated along the banks
are my fellow audience members of retired gawkers
in the cheap seats
passing snacks and cool drinks around,
taking in the show.

They say that in the muck being pulled up
are the lost gems and jewels that were once the cargo
of tall ships headed north to the wealthy in the 1800s,
some of them wrecked along the rocks and narrow passage
way,
giving up their bounty in a final soft landing,
the dark bottom becoming their silty case.

And the bounty waits still
for modern day plunderers to make their claims,
some from the deck of a river dredger
and some sitting in beach chairs,
happily wrecked by the sun and heat,
dreaming of vast fortunes,
pirates, one and all.

Drop and Roll

Saying good bye to my son and his girlfriend one day
after a visit to our place,
I ran back to the house for something I'd forgotten to give them,
and returning to their car
I misjudged the slope in the yard and started to fall.

That would have been surprising enough, but what really caused a scene
was that my old gymnastics chops kicked in from when I was a kid
and I landed a perfect tuck and roll, ending with legs apart, hands on my hips, glee in my heart.

Once the kids got past their shock that I hadn't been hurt,
came the truth they couldn't deny, nor myself, nor my husband,
the other witness of my feat.

They couldn't deny that at age 65, a slip and fall
did't mean I was ready for the home,
that I still had some moves
and that the old instincts were still there
for one more floor show,
loved by the judges who gave me a 10.
Nothing beats a 10 - it's perfect.
Nothing to change, nothing to fix.
It can't get any better than that.

R

Savoring

I can't sleep late anymore, the ability to do so having left me long ago.
After the last bathroom break, I follow the familiar urge to open the door
to my inner life and I'm called by music, stories, writing, or by paints
to create something, even before the sunlight reaches my window.

But first things first, I remind myself -
coffee, computer on, music selected, writing pad ready, art supplies at hand.
Then I sit at my desk and surrender to these early morning forces.

In some of my endeavors
I'm a co-creator with the muse I've come to know,
befriended and delighted by this inner artist.
In others I am a child,
happily lost in a world of make believe stories.

So delicious are these mornings,
so rich and refreshing,
they remind me of how lucky I am to live as I do,
marveling at the rewards of practice and hard work
and the small amounts of discipline
I've been able to squeeze out of myself,
still in grateful surprise at the payoff.

Then I take a sip,
savoring the richness,
watching another amazing sunrise outside my window,
all pink and promising.

S

Self-Sufficiency

I think it's only human to want to be good at something. The sense of self-worth that comes from a project well done can be immensely fulfilling and just the push a person needs to look forward to the next project. But if you're of the mindset that you need to reach your goals on your own, it's easy to set unrealistic expectations for yourself, creating the impossible demand that you get things right every time. For the self-sufficient person who's juggling a lot of balls, it's imperative to keep them all in the air at once with no room for mistakes. Because life is life, however, one will inevitably fall or the act will have to end for some unforeseen reason. And when it does, it can lead to an emotional crisis that's hard to get out of without the help of others that we all need sometimes.

If you think you have to go it alone in life and that you don't need someone in your corner who will support you when you're down, there's one thing you might consider - you could be colluding with the voices of oppression in your head. They may be telling you that:

- nobody else cares about what's happening like you do
- nobody else is as loyal you are
- nobody else gives as much as you do
- no one else will do it right

- you're the only one who can do it
- you might as well do it yourself

When it's you against the world like this, it keeps your connections with other people limited to "news, weather and sports." That shallow level of communication allows the self-sufficient person to "hit and run" - to take away what they need for themselves and disregard or minimize what someone else may need. It's all about them because they're all they've got.

Relationships like this can change in recovery. I've seen it many, many times with other people and in my own relationships. When a person becomes more mindful of others and of doing the next kind thing for someone else, it's no longer about whether or not they're giving too much or getting enough from the relationship. It becomes about something deeper and more meaningful; about giving because it's the right thing to do - with no strings attached.

Priorities change so that <u>to need</u> and <u>be needed</u> becomes the goal and reward. Worrying about keeping the balls in the air seems to fade away once the person begins to know themselves better and the boundaries they like to keep. They can just be themselves, comfortable with who they are. The way forward becomes clearer and broader because they're no longer relying solely on themselves.

I've learned that as strong and independent as I like to think I am, I still need help reasoning things out sometimes, and I've also learned that I don't have to drive myself crazy with something before I finally ask for the help. A lot of the time,

I can "take the foam off the latte," so to say, simply by talking about what's going on.

I attribute a great deal of my personal success to being able to reach out for guidance and feedback from other people. Going it alone doesn't work anymore, and that's a huge change in me, as a person who once thought she only had herself to rely on. Not today, and not ever again.

Shame

They're right. I'm too _(fill in the blank) _.

I don't deserve to have such a nice home.

I'm not smart enough for a job like this.

This is the voice of shame. It comes from the belief that you don't measure up, that you're inadequate, worthless, or weak. Shame is such a powerful emotion because it can crush a person's self-esteem with a single word, a look or gesture. The intensity of a shameful moment can often be recalled even many years later.

I think there's something insidious about shame that's hard to describe simply because of its slippery nature. There's an unpredictable sting and shock to it, like being caught off guard - a feeling that makes it hard to tell what's really happening. It's a set up for self-doubt that makes us ask ourselves, "What did I do wrong?" Then often comes, "What do they really think of me?"

When you're overwhelmed with the hurt of shame, your racing mind can be taken over by the banshees of shame, as I call them - those wailing voices in our minds, scaring us with scenarios of further humiliations to come. They can cause us to distrust other people and can be the source of anxiety that makes mountains out of a molehills.

I've learned the following guidelines that you may find helpful when shame comes your way:

166

- You can get good at seeing the wind up and the pitch of a "shame ball" that gets thrown at you by another person. Some of the sarcasm gets lost in translation in the following examples, but if you're familiar with these kind of mixed messages, you'll get it. For example,

   The wind up: "Thanks for <u>educating</u> me about this."
   The pitch: "I'm surprised that you know about something so complex."
   The wind up: "How nice of you to come by."
   The pitch: "I see that you don't call first."
   The wind up: "Oh, you must be hurt."
   The pitch: "I don't know <u>anyone</u> who's been hurt like <u>that</u>."

- Remember that it's your choice to let people into your life or not. For me, if I'm walking on eggshells around somebody who capitalizes on other people's embarrassment, it's a deal killer. I stay away. They don't deserve my time or attention.

- Remember that a person couldn't genuinely have your best interest at heart if they think it's ok to say hurtful things to you "for your own good." There's something else going on with that person that's not about you. You can simply say something like, "Thanks for the feedback," and let that shame ball fly right on by as you leave the scene. There's no need to lose your civility over someone else no matter how much their words have hurt you. It's not worth it.

- Some people project their own shame on to others through mocking and belittling words they think are funny. And if it happens to visibly hurt the one they've targeted, the person can also be mocked for feeling hurt. That cruelty is all about the shamer and the twisted ways they try to feel better about themselves - not about their targets. And while it might be educational to understand the motives of people who use shame like that, what becomes most important is to develop ways to detach and disengage from them because of it. It becomes vital to maintaining self-esteem because shame thrown around like that can destroy it.

In the end, it's just too much work to be around people who bite like that. I like straight talk instead, without the double meanings or snarky-ness that come with throwing shame balls.

So, today I try not to make things worse as a rule when it comes to these kinds of interaction by trying to avoid:

- Throwing back a shame ball of my own at the shamer
- Joining in a tit-for-tat or one-ups-manship to feel superior
- Telling myself that the hurtful thing they've said is ok when it's not
- Staying around for more when I should leave

Because I have people around me who don't throw shame balls, I'm aware if one comes out of left field in the course of a day. I'm also aware if I hear one being thrown at someone else. Life's too short to give any time to that kind of meanness. About a minute. That's all they get.

What <u>Healing</u> From Shame Looks Like

- Humility - in the silence of acting with dignity
- Compassion - by seeing yourself in others
- Kindness - in selfless giving, with no strings attached
- Responsibility - in the fulfillment of duty despite what others do
- Calm - in the steadiness of composure
- Forgiveness - in the acknowledgment of humanness
- Truth - in the knowing, and loving anyway

I get to see it every day in the examples of my friends. You know who you are. Thank you. Thank you.

The Solution - ACA

"The solution is to become
your own loving parent."*

Quite a statement. When I first heard someone say this at an ACA (Adult Children of Alcoholics) meeting over 30 years ago, I immediately said to myself, "That's too much - they're expecting too much." Despite being desperate for my life to change at the time, I was sure that to psychologically re-parent myself would be this huge, immense undertaking. I didn't know how or where to even start.

Up until then, I tried everything I knew to change the way things were going in my relationships, my roles, my work, my self...everything which in hindsight was basically advice from books. I did learn about healthier ways to live from the studying I did, but the truth is, I wanted a quick fix. I wanted magic. I wanted to blink my eyes and see before me the picture of the life I had always dreamed of. The idea that it would take time and action was depressing to me. I wanted SERENITY NOW, as the Seinfeldism goes.

I didn't know it then, but I was to learn over time that what was being offered to me in that ACA meeting wasn't a quick fix for my problems but a new way of life - of being responsible for myself and for my own growth. Learning that I didn't have to be rescued or fixed or changed by anyone else set me on a path of spiritual solutions where being my own parent could provide me with the direction I needed to make the changes I wanted in my life.

Through emotional pain that I thought might kill me some days, through radical changes in perception and through a spiritual revolution from my head to my heart, I came to know an inner guide - a soothing voice that calms me. From the steadiness of that calm, I was able to do an honest, deep dive into old negative thoughts and feelings that were affecting my daily life.

And from that place, I saw where I'd been wrong about certain things. I was able to recognize moments during my day when I was misreading what was actually going on between myself and someone else, the moments being colored by something - a thought or feeling - from the past. And after learning more about my own story, I saw that I had been driven by a need to control the people, places and things around me - control I was so sure I needed for everything to be all right, to be safe and the way it was supposed to be.

As a result of those lessons and more, I realized that I really only had control over my attitude and actions, so to face the fears and uncertainty of what just one 24 hour period could pose to me, I was going to need back-up. It was going to take being around other people who were seeking similar solutions to their problems. And being around them is where I found that spark of hope inside me and the desire to keep working for a better life.

Just as important as finding that part of my soul was learning that I had to commit to repeating words of encouragement to myself in troubled times - over and over again if necessary. It wasn't going to take a, "Calm down." I never learned how to calm down from that statement. It wasn't going to be, "Stop worrying." I never learned how to stop worrying from a statement like that.

From my inner loving parent, it was going to take a message of, "I hear you. I will be here with you no matter what" - and more loving sentiments repeated as many times as I needed. The solution, I found, was never to abandon myself again. And that has made all the difference.

* "The Twelve Steps of ACA (Adult Children of Alcoholics)," <u>Adult Children of Alcoholics,</u> ACA World Service Organization, 2006, pg. 108.

Spiritual Solutions

Sometimes I unwittingly dig deeper into an emotional wound to try to get relief from it. Not a good idea. To look for answers to a problem in the problem itself is how old thinking can still work against me and wear me down.

Similar to what I've shared earlier in this book, I've come to understand that the intensity of these emotional wounds can be triggered by an old core belief that says, "If it's intense, it must be true; it must be important." I can misread a situation, person or thing simply because of the intensity of the feelings attached to it. The chance for any rational thinking that the moment requires is lost because I can get hijacked by the strong physical reaction that comes with such feelings - tightened chest, clenched jaw, furrowed brow, short breaths, upset stomach, tearfulness, etc.

If I dig into the pain itself with continued self-hatred, self-criticism and maudlin memories, I just get more pain with no resolution at all. It only gives more energy to the old core beliefs of, "I'll never measure up," and "I deserve this pain," and on and on it goes. When I'm caught with those thoughts, I usually "get out the bat" to do a number of myself.

Wanting to change that tendency of being so hard on myself has lead me to use a scaling tool that helps me manage all of my feelings in general. I use it to gauge the intensity of a feeling so that I can see where I might be getting into trouble emotionally. The visual and an explanation follows.

The Scale

1 ————————————-5——————————10

The 8, 9, 10 range is the danger zone for me. I like to say "it's where my disease lives." It's the most intense, heightened way to experience a feeling. A lot of times the higher range is going to involve confusion, too. Exactly what's going literally and emotionally won't always be clear to me because of feeling overwhelmed. For example normal <u>anger</u> at about a 5 can morph into <u>rage</u> in that 8, 9 , 10 range; normal <u>sadness</u> at about a 5 can morph into <u>deep sorrow</u> in that high range. Five is good. It's where I can still feel the feeling and think rationally at the same time. I can reason things out in that zone. The 1, 2, 3 range can also be dangerous. It's where I'm avoiding something I don't want to think about or feel. It's there, but I want to deny it is - like a stone in my shoe that eventually has to be removed because it hurts so much.

I share a lot about using tools as part of recovery because I like to live in the solution - not the problem, and relying on the old ways I had of just pushing through a problem regardless of how hurt I was, or people pleasing regardless of how wrong it felt, just didn't work for me in recovery anymore. A more balanced inner life allows me to continue to grow and discover who I am, how the HP works in my life and how I might help someone else - all part of good spiritual life. Today, I understand my spiritual life to be that place where I find the power of love once again that can change regret into acceptance, anger into understanding, hatred into compassion, and so on.

S

The spiritual solutions to every day problems - big and small - are available to me when I can "stop, look and listen" to what's going on around me. Sometimes I can find the answer is in a simple gesture of kindness from someone else, a reading, in meditation, or in prayer. Sometimes all it takes is admitting I'm stumped by a problem and deciding to hand it off to the Universe. I've come to trust that an answer will circle back to me - sometimes quickly, sometimes slowly - in some way, shape or form that I hadn't seen before. That's when I send up a quick, "Thanks, Universe." I love those moments. And then there are times when, having let go of something, it'll be gone for good, only to notice at a much later date, in hindsight.

I refer to the different ways I handle life on life's terms as tools, but honestly, they're all gifts - gifts from growing with other people who also want to find solutions to their thinking and feeling problems. They have continued to share them with me for over 30 years now. Free of charge in the rooms of recovery.

Solutions await - not in some kind of A + B = C formula I thought I had to learn, but in a new way of life - a life that has room for both doubting and seeking, for letting go as well as holding tight to something.

May you find peace at the end of this day. May you find your process to get there, and may you share your story of healing with someone else. That completes the circle and makes you stronger for the next conflict that comes along - and the next opening in your soul for another spiritual solution.

175

The Stories We Tell Ourselves

Being kept in the dark about what's going on with your parents when you're a kid gets you good at making things up; at telling yourself stories to make sense of the way the adults act and why they do what they do. And even though it may be far from the reality of it all, the child will still believe their interpretation as if it's rock solid, holding onto it for dear life - out of fear and loyalty and love.

The story has to be true to the child because underneath the confusion and worry they carry is the small voice that says if things explode and someone gets hurt, <u>you</u> might get blamed for it. Hence, perfectionism. Hence, walking on eggshells. Hence, people pleasing, and so on. Kids have to believe their interpretation of the chaos and find a way to adapt to it because it's the best way they have to control it and make it seem manageable.

For a long time, I'd believed stories about my past to be 100% true. Fact. Then one day I decided to read over an old journal, and I discovered that for years I'd been using a timeline of events to blame myself for some things that couldn't possibly have been true. My assessment of what occurred was disjointed at best and showed that the beliefs I had about myself were more about low self-esteem than about anything factual. It was a revelation.

Since then, I've gotten in the habit of re-reading my previous writing - recent and older, and I'm awakened to a new insight into myself, often for the better, but sometimes I become aware of something I wish I hadn't. Stirring the pot of memories can be like that.

Regardless of what has been revealed to me about the stories I've carried and written, I've learned an important lesson that's formed the way I think about all writing. It's that our stories go on; they have no definite beginning and no definite ending.

The story continues, and what was changed or had been let go of is never really gone as long as I'm alive and able to remember it. It's all still a part of me, informing who I am today, this moment, for this story I'm writing right here. I can enter the story at any time, at any place. And I can leave it be. It's all up to me. The story is mine.

T

My Thoughts About Therapy

I had a career in the mental health field as a clinical social worker for 20 years and provided therapy to people with addictions and mental health diagnoses. I did it in intensive outpatient clinics, inpatient treatment, and as an individual therapist in private practice. I worked with alcoholics and addicts who had a variety of mental health disorders, many of them with dual diagnosis.

I worked with families, couples and children of alcoholic/ addicts. I taught a master's level course to social work students about addiction treatment. I held the positions of primary therapist in clinical settings, clinical supervisor to social workers in training and in practice, and I began a women's treatment program as a clinical director. As well, I never stopped attending recovery meetings for myself during my career.

As you can see, I've had a variety of work experiences plus many years in recovery that have lead me to draw some conclusions about the way I believe people think and why they seek mental health care. They follow.

- We each create our own personal set of guidelines and narratives about how to live our lives on a day-to-day basis. By an early age, probably 5 or 6, according to famous psychotherapist Alfred Adler, we have some general ideas about ourselves and the world.

- About self, it may be: I'm smart, I'm stupid, I'm successful, I'm pretty, I'm ugly, I'm a klutz, etc.

- About the world, it may be: people are nice, people are helpful, people are out to get me, people are to be used, other people are better than me, etc.

- From these we develop a style and pattern of living that's mostly consistent with these beliefs, such as: avoid failure at all cost, being in love means you have to make the other person the center of your world, don't ever forget who hurt you, always be charming, be the smartest one, be funny to make people like you, etc.

- As described by the British psychologist Frederic Bartlett and Swiss psychologist Jean Piaget in their theories of cognitive development, people formulate and apply schema to their experiences, schema being defined as the ways in which we unconsciously categorize and organize information in our minds. They become a solid foundation for what we believe is a true interpretation of the world. (This information is readily available through the internet. A great bibliography of their works can be found under their names in Wikipedia).

- These schema are formed at the time when we're limited by childhood logic and inexperience, and they become so ingrained into our thinking that I use the analogy of seeing the words that describe them deeply chiseled onto a cement wall in our brains. People become unconsciously loyal to ways of thinking and reacting because of those interpretations.

T

- What individual therapy can provide is a way of re-framing and re-defining the thinking and reacting that eventually brought the person to therapy. With willingness to learn new ways of thinking about their life and their future, change is possible, and therapy can provide the hope that comes with that change process.
- Trauma, addiction and serious mental health diagnoses add a dimension to therapy that requires evidence-based approaches and methods specific to the characteristic needs that accompany each of them. Providing therapy for people in those situations can be complex and often requires a comprehensive treatment plan with diverse therapeutic support.

For meaningful therapy to occur, regardless of the level of care they need, a person needs support, they need coaching, they need education, and they need kindness. I could offer that as a therapist, but what I couldn't offer was the willingness to take the action necessary to try out new ideas or accept the support. The willingness to even try has to come from within the person, from the taproot of who they, and hopefully, the support they receive opens the channel to what their motivations are for living.

It can be a game changer to have someone in your corner as you try living life on different terms than you once did. As a therapist, simply caring about how someone is feeling, helping them reason out their next move, or helping them heal from something that has already happened can be just what someone needs as the spark to change. The loneliness and isolation that comes with addiction and mental health issues are formidable, and whether or not a client of mine chose the path of change, it was an honor to shine a light on a possible way out. Many times I only planted seeds, and all I could do was hope that was enough.

If you're stuck in negative thoughts and feelings, if they keep coming around and you can't shake them, if you're dreading life and see no way out, get help.

Get therapy. It's the smart thing to do, and it may be the best thing you ever do for yourself, your family and the people you love. I know it was for me.

One More Tool
Forced Feeding Doesn't Work

One of my truths: I can't force feed new thoughts to myself if I'm still feeling hurt about something. Try as I might, if my feelings are raw and painful, say in the 8, 9, 10 range on the scale or in the needling irritation of a 2 or 3, I can only kid myself for so long about being over it. And the more I avoid feeling the pain all the way through - whatever that looks like - or the more I try to control it with a smile, with slogans or cajoling myself, the worse it eventually gets. I like the Buddhist saying: that which we avoid becomes stronger.

Trying to change my thoughts by force can look like this:

- being intellectual about an emotion - trying to explain it away
- being preoccupied with <u>why</u> I'm feeling something
- telling myself, "Get over it," "It happened a long time ago," "You're being over-dramatic," etc.
- repeating the same unconvincing message to myself only more forcefully

I know I can't force feed change to anyone else either. I can't control how a person thinks. I can't get inside their brain and mess with their neurotransmitters to have them experience the thoughts and feelings I want them to. Believe me. There were many times in my life I wish I could have had that power, but I only have human powers - not super powers.

I've learned that if I'm pushing a person to feel or think something they're not, we could both be missing out on one of the great moments in life where an immediate change in perception happens like a light switch being turned on - where they "see the light." Their thoughts suddenly connect to a new insight, and they begin to understand their problem from a different angle. It's a wonderful thing to see someone finally get it.

I know those kinds of experiences personally, and honestly, they haven't come about because I was badgered or prodded or pushed to think a certain way - by myself or someone else. Mostly, I believe, it's been from the patience I've shown myself and received from other people that makes walking through a maze of thoughts much more manageable. From a moment of kindness that can be as simple as being gently reminded to breathe, I can pause and reset myself towards what I can change and what I can't - the basis of all good solutions. Yes, kindness - positive personal regard, they called it in social work school - can be a powerful force for good in someone's life, proving to be the fertile moment for new thoughts to take hold for the next leg of their journey. Kindness - not forced feeding - does that.

Trauma

Trauma is a huge topic and one that for the purposes of this book, I'd like to keep simple and cover only the basics of what I've learned about it. I received trauma-informed training from Dr. Stephanie Covington, in Denver at CeDAR (Center for Dependence Addiction and Recovery) a treatment center where I was part of a team of doctors, therapists and nurses who provided inpatient care for people with substance use disorders and dual mental health diagnosis. I was also trained in the practice of EMDR (Eye Movement Desensitization and at Reprocessing), receiving my certification at The EMDR Center of the Rockies.

My experience has been that when most people think of trauma, they think of a one time exposure to an extraordinary and significant event. The DSM-V (The Diagnostic and Statistical Manual of Mental Disorders- 5th Edition), the diagnostic tool published by the American Psychiatric Association, states that the traumatic event leaves a person feeling powerless and having little control over their environment. Such events include natural disasters, situations they experienced in war, terrorism, a physical or sexual attack or catastrophic accident. In the field of study that addresses trauma and PTSD, Post Traumatic Stress Disorder, I learned a useful definition of these types of big events as "Big T" traumas. As outlined in the DSM-V, they include but are not limited to the symptoms of:

- Vivid flashbacks (feeling like the trauma is happening right now)
- Intrusive thoughts or images
- Nightmares
- Avoidance due to intense distress at a real or symbolic reminder of the trauma
- Physical sensations such as pain, sweating, nausea or trembling

In my studies of trauma in the broader field of trauma treatment, I've also learned that a person can be affected by an <u>accumulation </u>of smaller or less pronounced distressing events <u>over time</u> which can be extremely upsetting and cause significant emotional damage. These are referred to as "Little t" traumas and can include, but are not limited to:

- On going family conflicts
- Learning problems
- Long term health problems
- On going social relationship conflicts
- Infidelity
- Divorce
- Abrupt or extended relocation
- Legal trouble
- Financial worries or difficulty

Symptoms of "Little t" trauma can include but are not limited to:

- Flashbacks
- Confusion
- Difficulty focusing
- Not being able to make decisions
- Anxiety, depression

Multiple compounded and significant "Little t" experiences, especially if they occur in a short time span, can make life very difficult to navigate. These types of traumatic events may have occurred over the course of someone's life or they may be from the recent past.

Not everyone who's lived through "Big T" or "Little t" traumas experiences the symptoms of PTSD. There are a lot of factors that determine how a person is impacted by trauma, including their history of stress tolerance, their beliefs, perceptions, values and morals. But whether it's "Big T" or "Little t," it is the <u>avoidance </u>of addressing the emotional and psychic pain around the trauma that causes difficulties in functioning.

Avoidance can reach the point to where the individual is totally unaware of the impact of those experiences on their daily functioning. For the person experiencing "Big t" or "Little t" symptoms, it's hard to know what to do when one of the symptoms of the disorder - confusion - is the very thing you're experiencing in the moment. It makes it hard to know if it's time to ask for help. It makes you doubt yourself, causing you to think that you're weak and you should be able to get past the anxiety and sleeplessness. The confusion makes it easy to blame yourself for what happened.

It's easy to escape traumatic feelings and thoughts by using alcohol and drugs. It's also easy for medical professionals who are unaware of treatment options for PTSD to prescribe mood-altering, addictive drugs that do nothing but prolong a person's trauma symptoms and delay the therapeutic interventions needed to address them.

No matter what type of treatment you pursue with the help of a trauma-trained professional, this type of healing takes an on-going commitment to one's mental health. It's not a one and done thing. Some wounds run very deep and need time to mend. The traumatized brain (another huge topic which I won't address here) adapts and attaches to a kind of survival mode that can make life unbearable.

However, there is hope.

Trauma-based therapies can be very effective in treating trauma symptoms, the goal being to reduce their impact while at the same time using new ways of thinking and behaving that increase the quality of life. I found the reprocessing techniques of EMDR to be beneficial for some people caught in a web of frightening memories and hyper-vigilant reactions to triggers. I also found Narrative Exposure Therapy (NET) to be effective in developing a coherent autobiographical story for people struggling with fragmented memories. Having the logical beginning, middle and ending of a story instead of the bits and pieces of traumatic memory a person may have been carrying for a long time can be powerfully effective in reducing PTSD symptoms.

While there are no quick fixes for trauma, it's been my experience that when a person begins to address the emotional pain and distress of traumatic events, a spark of acknowledgement from deep within can lead to the necessary grieving, resolution and integration that changes lives. I have come to honor it as my own therapeutic process for continued healing from events that occurred in my life. I hope that everyone who reads this is motivated to find good mental health care if they're stuck in the maze of complex PTSD symptoms. Don't stop until you do. Heal and then tell someone else where to get help. That's how love works. Start with yourself.

(Excellent information re: trauma and PTSD can be found in the classic work, <u>The Body Keeps the Score: Brain, Mind and Body in the Healing of Trauma,</u> by Bessel van den Kolk, MD, 2014, available on <u>amazon.com</u>.)

True Confessions

A true story

I always wanted to have an accent other than the one that came with being from Cleveland, OH. I wanted to be different from everyone else around me, different from the conformists and the "sameness" that went along with attending St. Mary Magdalene Catholic School. We wore the same uniforms, the said the same prayers, practiced the same rituals, were given the same expectations by the nuns and priests. Different was good and it seemed to always catch my eye and ear whenever I saw it or heard it.

I liked the New York accent right away. It stood out so clearly different from mine. To me it said, "Hey - We are FAR from Cleveland and here is where everything big started - and we're the best, too!" To a little girl who wanted attention and to fit in somewhere new, it sounded exciting and full of possibilities.

My love of the differences in how we sound to each other didn't stop in NY, though. I loved musical phrases too.

My mom would make our school lunches in the morning to the sounds of her favorite radio station, and I would go to school with lyrics in my head like, "When the moon hits your eye like a big pizza pie..." or "Is that all there is?..." or "If I can make it there, I'm gonna make it anywhere, its up to you New York..." in my head all day, and sometimes out loud on the playground to whoever would listen - usually some dumbfounded fellow student who would just stare at me and most likely have thought, "OK - Now she's REALLY lost it".

My ear just naturally followed quirky sounds and I loved saying certain words and phrases. I would even put a towel on my head and pretend at home to be Sister Mary Leonardo (aka Sister Mary Charles Bronson) and sing in my best falsetto the responses in Latin from the mass, hitting my knees, eyes lifted in the prayerful reflection of a child in her elementary years, suddenly braking out in, "Et cum spìri tu tu o..."

And then...there was...French class! When I got to high school, I saw that everyone was choosing Spanish for their language requirement, but I joined the small group of students who chose French. Ahhh, France'...I think I caught the French bug early on when I saw that the same berets we wore to cover our heads at church were worn by the characters on TV who were supposed to be from France.

Growing up, my Mom worked in a bakery and brought home loaves of fresh Italian and French bread that we all loved. I remember no greater piece of toast than one made of fresh bread and fresh butter - mmmm. Learning that we had family members not only from Scotland and Ireland, but also from the Alsace-Lorraine region of France sealed the deal. I've been a Franco phile ever since childhood if for no for any other reason but the frenchy-ness of it. Oui...If only that accent was enough...

Unfortunately, my learning style for languages didn't allow for what was in a book or in the conjugations we did on the board. The distractions of high school and home would override the focus such a task demanded. Learning a new language at that time was a lot like what would happen with a very slow dimmer switch, never becoming quite bright enough to see how things fit together.

I found that the lights still burned a bit during a visit my husband and I took to Quebec several years ago. Well past the flexibility and focus it would take to actually learn the language, I was still surprised when a few words and phrases from that high school class came back to me. But with no discernible dialect, I fumbled for the most part, and in the end, was only comfortable with "ou sont les toiletes" ("Where is the toilet?"), and "jes sue enchante," (a formal, "Nice to meet you").

My husband, Jeff, had taken Latin in high school, and since there were no Romans around and I was baffled by the speed of this French I was hearing everywhere, he and I settled on saying the word "dumonde" to each other at the end of our sentences just to sound French, dumonde, meaning "the world" and having no logical use at the end of our French gibberish. We just liked pretending to fit in, and said things like, "Let's get chocolate croissants dumonde, or the car needs gas dumonde. Oh...if only the accent was enough...

Along those lines, our catch phrases for living in Naples, FL, seem to be seasonal, and after almost 5 years, I believe we speak a form of "Naplese." For instance, getting out of the car when returning home from somewhere during the tourist season, our go to phrase for squelching our inevitable complaints about the traffic is, "...but it's snowing in Denver!" or, "but it's 25 degrees in Cleveland!" And in the summer

T

when the heat is turning parking lots into frying pans, we say to each other, "Heat? What heat?," having vowed to never complain to each other about the temperature. Spoken like true natives...

Over the past few years, I've also become somewhat partial to "Talk Like Pirate Day" on every September 19th. I especially like saying "aaargh" as a general growl of unhappiness, and "Ahoy!" for hello. I like that there are accent lovers in the world with the same quirks I have. I imagine we're cut from the same cloth.

But the accent I loved the most, the one that I wanted to have so badly was an Irish accent. I wanted it so badly, in fact, that I tried it out once on a priest in confession one day at Church when I was in second grade.

I don't remember too well what my 7 year old reasoning was at the time, but I must have figured that in the confessional the priest would never know who I was, so I decided to give my faltering brogue a try, certain in the protection of the screen and his little sliding door.

Being new to the whole confession game, I didn't know or care about which priest I was getting. I was yet to learn which ones were nice and which ones threw the rosary at you, but I do remember being glad that he could only see the top of my head through the screen, being as small as I was. The anonymity was great.

So, I started, "Bless me father, for I have sinned..." and carried on in my 7 year old voice with a bunch of made up sins, trying to channel my long lost Irish relatives which sounded I'm sure like the curious conglomeration of a Clevelander,

TV shows, movies and the occasional missionary nun or priest who spoke at mass on an occasional Sunday.

When I finished, ready for my penance, instead of sticking to the script I had just learned in preparing for my first communion, the priest suddenly went OFF script and said to me through the screen in a sweet tone, "Oh, where are you from, dear?" Suddenly aware that I was actually telling a whopper by pretending to be someone I wasn't - in confession! - I was tongue-tied. I didn't know HE could even go off script.

My next move was evidence of the height of the decision-making skills I had at the time. I ran out of the confessional as fast as I could - of course, making a quick bow at the altar, then high tailing it out the side door, never to try to my powers on a priest again.

My love of the Irish accent has never left me. It sings to me still and calls to me to play with it and take it to my heart. I especially like the following prayer that seems to have the timing and cadence built right in to it:

May the road rise up to meet ya
May the wind always be at your back
May the sun shine warm upon your face.
May the rain fall soft upon your fields.
And until we meet again, may God hold you in the hollow of his hand.

True North

There's a point on a compass called "true north" that is aligned with the earth's axis. It's the line that goes straight from pole to pole. On my iPhone I can use the digital compass to see where I am in relation to it any time I want. I like that because I didn't always know which way I was pointed in life. For years, I followed the, "Well, THAT looks good," and "Let's go THAT way!" Plan for deciding the next right thing to do - even for big decisions, like where to live and with whom. It took several head bangings against several walls before I learned that my decision making needed some work. It took a while, but in time I learned to follow a few steps for making better decisions.

The first one is to gather information, and where I go to get that information is vital to the whole process. I had to admit to myself after yet another one of those head bangings that I could usually get a person to co-sign onto my impulsive, ill-conceived ideas as long as that person wasn't really invested in me or my life. The idea could be a really bad one, but if I asked someone who really didn't know me that well what <u>they</u> thought about it, they might just say what I wanted to hear, and then I was good to go. But asking for advice or feedback from a person who actually had my best interest at heart was a whole different matter. The honest realities and hard truths that someone else may see about the situation can be jarring, for sure, but they also be the information I need for the times I've been telling myself what I wanted to hear rather than what I needed to.

Next is making a "pro and con list" - right down to the practical and impractical. I just get it all out there. Making an honest assessment of whatever looks like it will work and what won't work is a great way to organize my thoughts and take some of the <u>foam off the latte</u>, so to say.

After that, I need to take action and follow through with whatever I decided was the right thing to do. It might involve making mistakes that are obvious right off the bat; other times I may have to wait and see what happens and reassess from there. Either way, however, I have to trust that in that moment it made sense. And if things don't turn out the way I wanted and I start using the baseball bat on my self-esteem again, I have to remember that to judge myself or anyone else with the hindsight of how things worked out for good or bad is being righteous and arrogant and something I try never to be. It's ugly.

My goal is to grow and evolve as a person right up to my last breath, and making impulsive, ill-conceived decisions is a waste of the time and energy I have left. When I remember that I'm not alone, that I have back up in my friends and family, and when I trust the wisdom I have to know the difference between what might work and what won't, then I can sense my inner compass pointed to true north in my world. It's a feeling of honesty and humility, both which come from the truth - unvarnished and raw at times, but straight and real. It's being in sync with myself. I know it when I have it, so I stick around in the company of other compass carriers, seeking the same. And that's a pretty great thing.

Unity

I've written a lot about what I've learned and how I've changed in this book, but I want to emphasize one idea that has made my life and my learning possible, and that is the concept of unity. Simply, it's that I can't do life alone. I've learned that we have to stick together if any of us are going to survive the calamities that life throws our way, and if we learn to do that, the enjoyment and sheer beauty of the experience has a chance to unfold. I've experienced the richness of a life very worth living because I am part of the bigger picture of how it connects to others. By taking the actions of service and support of another person, I believe we simultaneously allow ourselves to give and be given to in ways that heal us. The wounds from childhood become transformed. The wounds from our own bad choices are healed.

As a traveler in the Universe, sometimes I have to tighten my seatbelt, but I'm here for wherever the ride takes me, next to my fellow travelers, grateful for the long, strange trip so far, ready for what's around the corner. Come what may.

Getting Unstuck:
A Journey Through Fear

Fear, worry, anxiety, and guilt. Those feelings make up the perfect storm for what it's like to be overwhelmed for me. I've had a long relationship with these feelings and understand their corrosive thread throughout my life. I've also come to understand that the source of much overwhelm and low level panic was the fear that something bad was happening right now or was going to happen in the future that I'm just not be aware of, that I could be missing. It's like constantly waiting for the other shoe to drop, no doubt written on the wall of my psyche during my childhood.

The solution to living with this and other fears in my young mind was to be prepared, or hyper-prepared, actually, with a vigilance that colored my early years with tension, worry, and anxiety. I was desperate for my mother and siblings to be happy and safe in our unpredictable home. I thought it was smart to be prepared for the chaos my father might create, and the way I did this was mainly through trying to be perfect. To me it made sense that if everything could be just so, if I looked a certain way, or the house did, or if whatever I was doing at the time was the best, then everything would be ok. It was the attempt of a child to control the uncontrollable - to have power over something where she had none.

This solution, of course, was no solution at all, and it lead me to a life of fear, worry and anxiety - a mindset that always kept me on the look out for trouble. It was also a source of low self-worth in my life, due in large part to the impossibility of meeting the high standards for beauty and achievement that I had for myself, standards mostly from books, movies and TV, that were a set up for the result of never feeling like I measured up.

I constantly compared myself to others I believed to be better than me and tried to be like them. As a good cover up, I had a measure of bravado and pride to pull me through a lot of the fear, but making life decisions based on fear left little room for developing an inner life or for any self-awareness to take hold. If you liked me, that was enough for me to like me, and the fear that you might not some day ran my life and relationships.

I eventually came to a turning point about fear during my first sober summer home with the kids. I had been sober about 9 months by then and my routine of meetings, coffee with people, meeting with my sponsor was going to change. I was a wreck about it, still not having worked through how to handle fear and anxiety. I had given my kids which was to me a perfect-looking, idyllic life, but I didn't know how I was going to handle the changes ahead from this new life in sobriety I had created for myself during the 9 months they had been in school.

What eventually worked was to make small changes where I could at first. I changed small things in my daily routine to adjust to having them home. We lived in a neighborhood with a lot of kids, so my plan was to get a sitter every day to be able to still go to meetings. I also took the kids to a local salad bar every day so I could get out of the kitchen,

I took them to the local amusement part (a lot!) or to our beach every day, gardening (a lot).

Soon I saw the bigger changes coming to fruition. I was feeling more comfortable in my own skin, I was laughing a lot more, I was slowing down and enjoying my home and the kids, watching them grow up right before my eyes. Every once in a while I would have these spiritual awakenings in moments when I could breathe and see that everything was good. I was handling sobriety.

I was surprised to find that by having worked my program, I had enough "insurance" built up that afforded me to be flexible in the ways I was going to keep my sobriety on the front burner. I found I was building courage and self-esteem again by making these smaller changes in my routine that afforded me to see a way forward through the fears, anxiety and depression that had followed me for so long.

It took action - not the crazy, frenetic, impulsive action of anxiety, but action that included self-care, self-reflection, time with recovering women - not at all what I had pictured sobriety would be like. I was so afraid that my life would blow up when I got sober - that I'd be divorced, that I'd lose my kids, my home, etc. - but I didn't. Maintaining my sobriety was going to take a series of small, consistent changes with a willingness to keep going, and by the grace of a Creator that wants only good for me, I was given it and still am to this day.

With these new, positive experiences in recovery, I gained perspective on what emotional sobriety is and what it felt like to be balanced on the inside - to be able to make better decisions and care for myself and my family. I learned that fear is just another emotion - one to be felt and not avoided (that only makes it worse), to be accepted for what it is and offer it up to the Universe for whatever the lesson is to be, and then take action to keep moving forward.

When I follow that process, my thinking always improves and I get out of the emotional jackpots that used to lead me to more fear and depression and eventually to a drink. I used to tell myself it was helping me relax and think things through, but instead, it took an awful toll on me.

I have a friend who says, "Move a muscle, change a thought." In other words, taking action when you're stuck - maybe especially with fear - will allow you to make room for new thinking. I believe that's how we're made as humans- that our bodies are made to move and our minds are designed to create and learn.

I sincerely hope if you're feeling emotionally stuck that you find your own process to get unstuck and into a life you can live on life's terms - not one dictated by old beliefs and fears. Get unstuck - life's too sweet to stay there.

V

Valuing This Moment

From <u>The Language of Letting Go</u>, by Melodie Beattie, p. 234

"This moment, we are right where we need to be, right where we are meant to be. How often we waste our time and energy wishing we were someone else, were doing something else, or were someplace else. We may wish our present circumstances were different.

We needlessly confuse ourselves and divert our energy by thinking that our present is a mistake. But we are right where we need to be for now. Our feelings, thoughts, circumstances, challenges, tasks - all of it is on schedule. We spoil the beauty of the present moment by wishing for something else.

Come back home to yourself. Come back home to the present moment. We will not change things by escaping or leaving the moment. We will change things by surrendering to and accepting the moment.

Some moments are easier to accept than others.

To trust the process, to trust all of it, without hanging on to the past or peering too far into the future, requires a great deal of faith. Surrender to the moment. If you're feeling angry, get mad. If you're setting a boundary, dive into that. If you're grieving, grieve. Get into it. Step where instinct leads. If you're waiting, wait. If you have a task, throw yourself into the work. Get into the moment; the moment is right.

We are where we are, and it's okay. It is right where we're meant to be to get where we're going tomorrow. And that place will be good."

These words changed me. They gave me just what I needed at the right moment to calm and soothe myself; to take a breath, look at the beauty around and just be. Dots connected for me as a young mom early in sobriety, when I read this one morning, eager for a better life for my self and my kids, and wanting to change everything at once. I learned that change wasn't going to happen because I frantically kept the pulse of everything that was happening. It was going to come by stopping, looking and listening - just like a little kid. It was going to take trusting that one moment held enough for now - that it held a much greater power than I could ever understand; a power greater than me.

The growth I was seeking was going to come one day, one hour, one minute, one moment at a time. And I learned that was enough for changes - big ones - to happen. Just one moment at a time. After all, there was one moment in my life when I was certain I couldn't get off the merry-go-round I was on, and then I did and that was the greatest change of all.

W

God's Will

When I still thought like a second-grader about spiritual matters and prayed to God like God was Santa Claus, I believed I was always doing it wrong. It felt like I could never guess what God's will for me actually was. I heard a lot about it growing up, of course. I heard that God knows everything, including the future, and that I just had to figure out what He expected from me. I thought if I could decipher God's code, then I'd know what to do and all would be well.

I held this confusing belief about how God worked until I began developing an adult, open-minded spiritual life without judgement or contempt. And when I did, all of that changed. I changed, and I experienced a conversion of sorts, in an a-haa moment when one day I read a simple suggestion in recovery literature from a man who had similar thinking as I did. He suggested that all I had to do was the next right thing in front of me to be done, and however it turned out, THAT was God's will for me.

That meant I didn't have to <u>know it before I acted</u>. It turned out that what I thought was God's message to me about what to do next was just me talking to me, not God talking to me. I had to admit I had been wrong about spiritual matters and that I'd been acting like a mini-God for myself, telling me what I wanted to hear - be it loving or harsh. I was still guessing like I had in second grade.

So, today, I still follow the suggestion to do the next right thing and leave the results up to God, the Universe, Creator, etc. Oh, sure - I can still get caught up in worrying about the future sometimes and what to do about it. My kids live far away - that alone can be a source of worry. It seems that a lot of people don't want to play by the basic societal rules we've lived and worked within as a society for a long, long time - that can be a source of worry, too.

But I don't stay there too long. I have the wisdom to know the difference between what I need to accept and what I can do something about, and I know how to keep it simple by doing the next right thing, the next kind thing in front of me that needs to be done. I also have the wisdom today to know I can't control the way things are going to turn out. I might get it right sometimes, but that's only a lucky guess in the end.

If I do this, day after day, I find I have a new understanding of who and what God is to me today. I have an evolving relationship with that God, that Higher Power, the Universe, the Spirit that I try to let time unfold without gumming it up. If I do that, I can see how long ago the second grade was and I'm grateful for it. Every day.

X

EXamples

I once heard a well-known basketball player say with disgust, "I'm not ANYBODY'S role model!," and I thought yes, you are. You just don't know it.

We all stand for something - some belief, for a way of life, for some principle. It's represented by our actions and how we live our daily lives, and for those of us who have chosen to get sober and stay sober, we stand for the possibility of change. We say that you can break the cycle of addiction in your life. We are examples of how to be your best self without altering your mind or your mood. And the best thing is that we get to stand for these things as examples for our children, our family members, our employers, our co-workers, our friends.

And sometimes it's being an example to someone you randomly meet in a coffee shop or at the dry cleaner or the gas station. We get to be good examples to neighbors and acquaintances anywhere we go, and people notice. It's attractive. When you're genuinely happy, it comes through to other people, and that's no small thing in the world today.

We volunteer for this life in recovery. No one can make you do it, not for long anyway. We volunteer to begin a new way of life and we get to be good examples of how to live it. The riches from this choice are too many to name. I've written an alphabet book to give it a try. One letter at a time.

Y

You

I hope you've been able to identify with some things I've written in this book and that it's been helpful to you. I also hope it may help <u>you</u> help someone else just as I was when these ideas were handed to me over time. To pass along the good we experience in recovery is something not to be missed, and I'm so grateful for the chance to have done that. If you can do that for someone else because of one thing I've written, that would be the greatest gift I could ever get from this work... and I learned that from people like you.

Z

"It's ok to have zero f***s left."

I learned from some amazing women in my life that it's ok to stop giving energy to a person, place, thing or situation that's sucking the air out of it. It's ok:

- to come to a full stop and say "No."
- to say "Enough is enough."
- to leave the room
- to stop blowing up your life because of a relationship that's not working
- to make a big change in your life
- to feel differently than the way you felt yesterday, or this morning
- to change your mind
- to say it's too late
- to want something else
- to have zero f***s left to give.

Many thanks and much love, Zeroes. ♥